The Saga of Rickshaw

Identity, Struggle and Claims

Sarokar / A Series

The Saga of Rickshaw

Identity, Struggle and Claims

A Study by Lokayan

Editor: Rajendra Ravi

VĀK

INSTITUTE FOR DEMOCRACY AND SUSTAINABILITY

लोकायन Lokayan

CENTRE FOR THE STUDY OF DEVELOPING SOCIETIES

ISBN : 978-81-8143-412-8

VĀK

21-A, Daryaganj

New Delhi- 110002

First Edition : 2006

Cover : Pradeep Saha

S.N. Printers, Delhi-110032

Rs. : 200.00
$: 9.95

THE SAGA OF RICKSHAW
Edited by : Rajendra Ravi

Edited by
Rajendra Ravi

Written by
Radheshyam Mangolpuri

Re-written by
Abhay Kumar Dubey

Translated by
Avinash Kumar
Ruchi Kaushik

Researched by
Smita Snehi
Dhananjay Kumar Singh

Graphics by
Sanjeev Shashwati

Photographs
National Gandhi Museum, New Delhi
Jawaharlal Nehru Museum and Library, New Delhi

Sarokar / A Series

The ***Sarokar / A Series*** *published under the auspices of the* ***Indian Languages Programme*** *of the* ***Centre for the Study of Developing Societies (CSDS)*** *aims at focusing on those aspects of social reality, which are rendered almost invisible in various political and discursive meta-narratives. The politics of knowledge working hand in glove under the new and old structures of capital and elitism try its level best to throw these realities out of focus. They have left no stone unturned to keep them off the priorities of modernisation, urbanisation and globalisation. The primary target of this series is to highlight these subdued shades of reality. This series invites all those studies, reports, surveys, analyses and the other factorial details by all the alert activists, intellectuals and organizations who wish to draw the marginalised realities towards the centre of academic discussions.*

Dedication

*To the vibrant urban poor who
does not lose heart from the difficulties
borne out of poverty and displacement, who
has to constantly work against all odds
of an unjust governance, who considers
rickshaw-driving as one of the many
respectable jobs and offers active contribution
to the economic, social, ecological
and transport sectors.*

In Gratitude

This book is entirely based upon the study known as 'Action Research Programme on Rickshaw and Rickshaw-pullers 2000-2002' and contains a survey of those people whose lives have been organised around the rickshaw, that is rickshaw-drivers, owners, mechanics, manufacturers, unions and passengers. We are extremely grateful to the surveyed people who never hesitated to co-operate in our efforts. Several socio-political activists, social scientists, litterateurs, artists, TV and print journalists, environmentalists, technologists, transport policy experts, administrators and general citizens have also time and again chipped in to make this difficult and time consuming task a little easier for us. We are especially indebted to honorary advisers of this project: Dr. Ajit Jha, Dr. Onkar Mittal, Dr. Gitam Tiwari, Dr. Ritu Priya, Dr. Y.P. Anand, Prof. Imrana Qadir, Prof. Imtiaz Ahmad, Prof. Dinesh Mohan, Prof. Dheerubhai Sheth, Prof. V.B. Singh, Arun Kumar, Prashant Bhooshan, Yogendra Yadav, Vijay Pratap and Smitu Kothary. They throughout maintained the process of their creative interventions at every stage of the study. Financial help came from TRIP, IIT, New Delhi and from the Institute for Democracy and Sustainability without which this publication couldn't have seen the light of the day. The study was made possible due to the funding from Sir Dorabji Tata Trust, Mumbai. Besides, we really do not know how to express our gratitude for innumerable persons and many institutions that provided a helping hand in completing and writing this document and making it aesthetically appealing.

contents

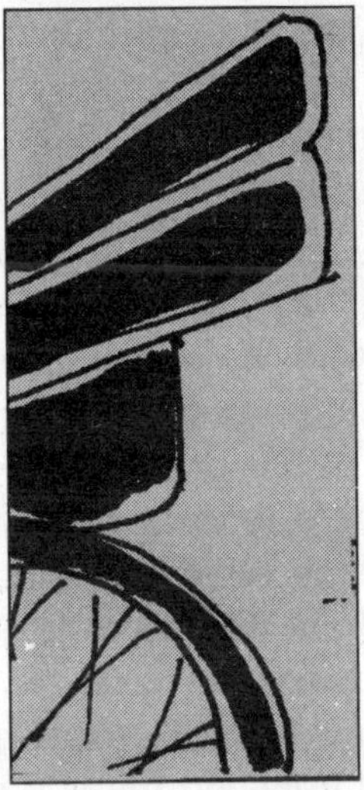

Editor's Note

The Place of Rickshaw in a Democracy

Rajendra Ravi

We have been interacting with displaced labourers in Delhi for the last 15 years. We got in touch with them in almost every field of their activity. In the beginning, they did not welcome us very warmly and used to tell us that they were not interested in general issues. Later, when we began to talk about the issues related to their lives, they got interested in our work.

While taking the initiative on the Mandal Commission Representation Bill in 1989, we got close to rickshaw-drivers. Earlier, we considered the profession of rickshaw driving as extremely inhuman. We were in favour of banning rickshaws. But later our close relationship with the rickshaw-drivers made us aware of the importance of rickshaw driving.

After this, we began to be associated with their issues. We organised a meeting in which rickshaw-owners also participated. They too raised some specific issues and told us that without paying attention to the problems of rickshaw-owners, it would not be possible to resolve the problems of rickshaw-drivers. We also felt that they were right. When we began to support the rickshaw-owners, we had to face criticism from several quarters. In 1998, we organised a meeting of rickshaw-owners and rickshaw-drivers at Gandhi Peace Foundation. Rickshaw-drivers, rickshaw-owners, educationists, policy makers, social activists and other intellectuals active in different fields participated in this meet. There was a positive change in their viewpoint regarding the business of rickshaw after this meet.

The cycle-rickshaw of NCR (National Capital Region) is not merely a mode of transport nor is it only a last support for the livelihood of the poor man. Rather, in today's context it is a symbol around which the entire story of the democratic development of India organises itself with its own reality. Not only employment and honour can be restored to the poor man by doing justice to the rickshaw but a base for the creation of a healthy society can also be prepared as well. The rickshaw protects our environment, contributes to our economy and despite all its wretchedness, helps in defending the self-respect of a poor citizen called the rickshaw-driver. The results indicated by our study centred on the rickshaw of NCR and people associated with this profession support this conception.

All the people associated with the rickshaw business are either poor or with very little capital. The rickshaw-driver is that urban poor, who either belongs to this very region or has come here from any town or village of this country in search of better employment and not finding any job or the job of his choice or having been evicted out of a job, has resorted to driving a rickshaw. The results of liberalisation and globalisation have become apparent in a very short span of time. There is no area within the NCR, which hasn't faced the wrath of liberalisation. Factories have closed down on a large-scale in this area. With the increasing hegemony of the products of MNCs in the country, the demand for national products has almost gone down completely. Both our indigenous industry and agriculture have been destroyed. Those industries that escaped were forced to close down in the name of restoring the environment of the city. Lakhs of people have been unemployed with these closures. A large number of these turned towards the rickshaw and are somehow making their living through it. Most of them are driving rickshaws; a few are managing as owners or mechanics. Similarly, those dispossessed by the feudal oppression in the countryside or having lost their jobs due to the mechanisation of agriculture have come to the city and are making ends meet with the help of a rickshaw.

Voices of these poor often echo in my ears, 'We are poor out here, but not slaves. We were both poor and slaves in the village'. The other person says, 'We came here in search of work from the village. There is no work there and even if we find it sometimes, wages are quite low. Second, the master keeps abusing and humiliating us at the slightest pretex.' Compare it with what another rickshaw-driver has to say, 'This is the ideal job with complete freedom. If I feel like it then I drive the rickshaw otherwise simply rest. If I don't feel like it, I can simply say no to the passenger. I am talking to you right now. I can talk for an hour or two. Can any master give me any opportunity or time to talk like this? Never!'

Having lost their jobs through the closure of industries, people had not even settled down when their slums began to be destroyed. This happened in the name of making roads or the Metro rail or green belt or a plush shopping centre or office or some other post-modern building. Either no alternative arrangements were made to rehabilitate them or they were thrown out so far from the city where there was no possibility of earning livelihood through rickshaw. Their wives lost their jobs of housemaids. In some ways, they have been placed back into the same misery because of which they had left their villages. A 'basti', which we had visited during our survey, was missing on our second visit. The bulldozer had trampled everything. We don't know where those owners, mechanics, rickshaw-drivers went, who while talking to us felt secure in saying : 'If we have got rickshaw, we will battle out the bigger hurdles of life merrily.' When it was a painful experience for us, you can imagine what they must have gone through.

Roads are being widened in the NCR with great aplomb these days. Flyovers and subways are being constructed on various different roads. But no consideration is being given to the slower vehicles during their construction. The rickshaw too is a public transport but the planners of the city and the engineers engaged in construction don't think that way. The rickshaw and other slower vehicles are culprits in their eyes; hence they consider it appropriate to push them out of the roads. But what is the reality? The government has given unlimited permission to motorised private transport (scooters, motor cycles, cars, etc.) The result is that tens of thousands of such vehicles are increasing every month. On the other hand, control is being imposed through licensing on the non-motorised vehicles, which include the rickshaws. Not only this but roads are being banned for them on a large scale in Delhi. The roads where they are allowed to ply don't have separate lanes for them. The problem of air pollution due to the increasing crowd of motorised vehicles is becoming alarming day by day. But our government can come up with only one solution—to run motor-driven public vehicles on CNG. The orders of the Supreme Court are helping fully in making the intentions of the government operational. Hence the diesel-run government buses have been removed from the roads in Delhi. Due to this, it has become impossible for rickshaw-drivers living in far-off rehabilitated zones or any other person to come to the densely populated zones for their livelihoods. Rickshaw-drivers and the citizens living in the city are fed up with inhaling the smoke of the motor vehicles and are falling sick with different ailments. A rickshaw-passenger comments about the 'transport policy', 'Our transport policy is decided by car-manufacturing MNCs. They see the solution of traffic jams in the increase in the number of roads, their widening, construction of flyovers on them and exit of traditional and public transport from the roads. The result is that our government prepares the budget only with the purpose of providing convenience to the vehicles used by the affluent section and even gives them legal protection. In practice, it neither helps in resolving the issue of jams nor of pollution.' Another passenger says, 'Cars are no more modes of transport, rather of displaying wealth. Four members of the same family use four cars to reach the same office while they can do the same with only one. If they are concerned about society then they can also give lift to people going in the same direction—they can even charge fare from them. It will help in many ways: there will be less possibility of traffic jams, it will lead to conservation of fuel; it will also help in saving foreign currency; protect environment, people will reach their destination on time, feeling of mutual cooperation will grow and there will be sufficient space for non-motorised vehicles on the roads.'

The issue of space for non-motorised vehicles is not an issue of somebody's magnanimity; rather it is the right of every person using the roads that his/her vehicle should get equal freedom to ply on the roads. Only a 'unified transport policy' can provide a solution to the problems of jams, pollution and accidents etc. related to the roads. A 'transport policy' evolved with an eye on all modes of transport will strengthen democracy on the road. The number of different vehicles in accordance with the needs as well as restrictions on them will be placed through this. Thus it would not be possible to give a free signal to motorised vehicles and a bar on transports like rickshaw. The manifestation of today's transport policy is that motorised vehicles remain in jams for hours and literally crawl. A man walking on foot covers a short-distance journey quicker than a car. The best transport policy is that which gives maximum support to public transport and desists the tendency to keep personal vehicles. Only then the useless expenditure of millions-trillions of rupees on unnecessary construction will be utilised for the generation of employment for the people. Then perhaps so many people would not be forced to look towards the rickshaw. The declaration of rickshaw as illegitimate has also contributed in creating major hurdles for its technical progress and maintenance. Whereas new models of cars, etc. hit the road every six weeks, the rickshaw is running on the same pattern for many years. No rickshaw-producer is ready for any new experiment because no rickshaw-driver or owner wants to spend extra money on it and even the rules-regulations of the municipal councils don't permit any change in size or appearance of the rickshaw. Despite all this, if there is some aesthetic variation in the rickshaws of different places, it is all due to the inner strength of risk-taking on behalf of the rickshaw-drivers and owners. Why would any owner spend extra money in decorating and maintaining his rickshaw when the administration has issued orders to impound and destroy it? The maximum cost of this system is borne by the rickshaw-driver. He has to remain with that machine which provides him his meal at the expense of damaging his health. Only an openhearted acceptance of rickshaw as a public transport by the government can make its technical development possible. Countries conscious of environmental issues are giving special attention to bicycles and rickshaws in their transport system. They are also spending a lot of money on the research for the progress in its technology. They are even providing money to other countries for this kind of research.

It is indeed unfortunate that our government is not serious about even the the environment. Even the courts saddled with the problem of the environment apply double standards. Both the government and courts don't treat all the citizens of NCR on an equal basis. In the name of making Delhi pollution free they initiate strict action to evict diesel run public vehicles like buses, three wheelers and taxis out of Delhi. Yet they don't bother in the least about those cities where these vehicles seek refuge. Those vehicles evicted out of Delhi are freely plying in Ghaziabad, Loni, Noida and Meerut etc. One rickshaw-owner in Meerut asks, 'Are the people of Meerut pollution-proof? Is there any difference in the structure of their lungs and Delhiwallahs' lungs? If not, then why such step-brotherly treatment?' Then he answers in the same vein as if unravelling a mystery, 'Nobody is bothered about pollution, not even Delhi pollution. If that had been the case private vehicles would have been converted to CNG in the first place. How many public vehicles (in Delhi) ply on CNG? Only a few thousand. It has made very little difference to the pollution, not even one per cent. But almost 40 lakh private vehicles are running on Delhi roads. Isn't their smoke spreading pollution? But no, banning them would have led to somebody's displeasure. Actually the market forces are dreaming of establishing a city full of luxury for their consumers by pushing out common men.'

Hence people from other areas of NCR are looking suspiciously at Delhi. The plying of evicted vehicles in these cities has not only led to an increase in air and sound pollution, it has also affected the rickshaw business. The income of rickshaw-drivers and owners has fallen back because now they are finding fewer passengers. There is also talk of controlling the numbers of rickshaws in Meerut by the administration. It is being said that the increase in numbers of rickshaws has led to the problem of traffic jams in the city. Even the bigger among rickshaw-owners of Meerut and Rohtak are raising the issue of controlling the number of rickshaws, hence a contradiction is emerging in the rickshaw-business from within. Those already entrenched it fear that with the coming of new people their business will collapse. At this juncture, the transport system doesn't remain an independent unit, rather it becomes a part of the entire economic system. Hence it seems necessary that if Delhi is to be saved then we have to ponder over the plan for the entire country. If people get necessary facilities and employment in their own area or around it then why would they need to run over to any far off city hundreds of kilo metres away?

This might sound quite a distant thing to our planners. At present, at least this much is needed that rickshaws be considered as part of public transport and a means of livelihood and be given the right place in this democratic structure. But even this would not be possible easily. The rickshaw-driver, owner, mechanic or producer, whoever has attained something from the government or society, has had to resort to the path of struggle. Without their unity, this struggle was neither possible in the past nor will it be in the future. There is a need for an ideological awakening for this struggle. The people in the rickshaw-business belong to the unorganised sector. Hence a continuous pedagogy is needed to awaken them. They will have to be given information about their rights, duties and rules of traffic. Non-governmental organisations like Jan Parivahan Panchayat, Lokayan can provide one source of information for this work. They can bring planners, officials of municipal bodies, officials of traffic police, specialists from the society, social activists and the people from the rickshaw-business on one forum and create a common understanding between them. As far as the issue of creating organisational unity and leadership among the people of the rickshaw-business is concerned, only people of this very community can do it.

The aim of our book is to place the real conditions of the people associated with all the aspects of the rickshaw before the common people. This book is a document about the cycle-rickshaw of NCR. This document will help in changing the lives of people associated with the rickshaw-business. We firmly believe in this.

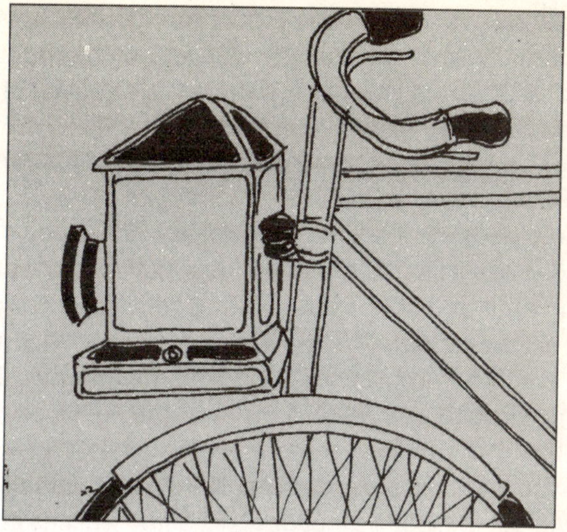

The Survey

A Few Things about the Methodology

'The Saga of Rickshaw' is an attempt to bring forth all the aspects associated with the rickshaw-business in the National Capital Region. This book is based on facts, information and data presented in the survey titled 'Action Research Programme on Rickshaw and Rickshaw-drivers 2000-2002' conducted by Jan Parivahan Panchayat, Lokayan. A thorough investigation has been made into the social, economic, health and work related conditions associated with the rickshaw-drivers, rickshaw-mechanics, owners renting out their rickshaws, rickshaw-producers, rickshaw-unions and passengers commuting through the rickshaws. For this we interviewed concerned people through a questionnaire and also talked to them informally. Meetings were held with the rickshaw-producers as well as specialists of rickshaw-technology. Views of social activists, political representatives, union leaders and officials of the municipal bodies and the officials of the traffic police were also taken.

A glance over the sample size chosen for the survey makes it clear that the goal of the study was to reach a group that can reflect the broadest representation, which could truly present the picture of the rickshaw-business not only on an individual basis but also as an important segment of the unorganised sector.

The biggest problem associated with the study of the rickshaw business was that selection of related persons couldn't be made on an impromptu basis while conducting a survey. There was no such source available with the surveyors to make this kind of a selection possible. There was neither any data available on the people related to the rickshaw-business from any industrial survey nor was there any existence of a category like the rickshaw in any other census. It was also virtually impossible to find out the exact number of rickshaw-wallahs in the entire region. Investigations about rickshaw-wallahs were carried out in government departments of the region, questions were asked in the offices of the municipal bodies and the information was collected from traffic police and rickshaw-owners to find out their exact number. We have not been able to collect data from all the areas of the region. Our study is based only on 24 towns. How many rickshaw-drivers applied for licenses in these towns of the region and how many of them got it—these numbers were figured out on the basis of this data. An idea of these figures can be had from the table 1.

It is clear from table 2 how big the difference between the total number of the rickshaw-drivers in the region and the license-holding rickshaw-drivers is. Yet, despite the authenticity of the sources, only the number of licensed rickshaws can be believed and not the number of the rickshaws without license. The reason is that everywhere the surveyors felt that the attitude of the administration was that of an opportunist. For example, if the administration would be involved in the drive to impound the rickshaws then it would present highly exaggerated data and if it was cornered on the tendency of not giving enough licenses then it would come up with less numbers. Anyway, in the context of such tactics of the administration when the surveyors collated the governmental and non-governmental assumptions then it was estimated that at least 6 lakh rickshaw-drivers are eking out their livelihood through the rickshaw in the region. An estimated 4,69,220 rickshaws exist supposedly in the 24 townships alone.

Table-1 / Sample of Survey

No	Region	Driver	Owner	Passenger	Mechanic	Total
A	**Haryana**					
	Bahadurgarh	21	3	3	2	29
	Faridabad	440	59	58	30	587
	Palval	21	3	3	2	29
	Hodal	10	5	5	5	25
	Gurgaon	271	37	38	17	363
	Sohna	10	5	5	5	25
	Sonipat	34	4	4	3	45
	Panipat	39	5	5	3	52
	Rohtak	34	4	4	3	45
	Rewari	45	6	6	3	60
	Dharuhera	2	—	5	5	12
B	**UP**					
	Ghaziabad	249	35	36	18	338
	Loni	10	5	5	5	25
	Modinagar	10	5	5	5	25
	Muradnagar	12	5	5	5	27
	Noida	70	9	8	5	92
	Dadri	10	5	5	5	25
	Meerut	393	52	52	26	523
	Hapur	45	6	6	3	60
	Bulandshahar	45	6	6	3	60
	Khurja	24	3	3	2	32
C	**Rajasthan**					
	Alwar	79	10	10	5	104
	Bhiwari	8	1	5	5	19
D	**Delhi**	**396**	**35**	**36**	**24**	**491**
	Total	**2278**	**308**	**318**	**189**	**3093**

[illegible] ample given in the table 1 that the maximum [illegible] urvey is on rickshaw-drivers. Their repre[illegible] um (2,278) in this respect. From the point of [illegible], the number of passengers using the rickshaw [illegible] mber of people plying it. Even in the sample their [illegible] econd, i.e. 318, though it might seem as if their rep[illegible] on is not enough. There is a need to understand the natu[illegible] and context of the survey at this juncture. The view of the customers in bringing out various aspects of the rickshaw-drivers is important yet only secondary.

A glance at the questions asked during the survey also tells about the different aspects of the lives of rickshaw-drivers that were touched upon. Among the 102 questions asked were their age, caste, religion, education and marital status. Later they were asked where they came from originally, how did they live in NCR—alone or with the family, do their wives also work, if yes then what kind of work they did, did their children go to school, what had been their traditional family vocation, what was the reason behind their migration to the region, what did they do in the village, why did they have to leave the village, did they go back to the village to do some other work, if yes then what, what were the benefits of coming to the city, what kind of problems did they have to face out here, how did the people behave with them normally, where did they live, where did they get the drinking water from, where did they go to defecate, how did they get electricity, what kind of fuel did they use to cook, did they have ration cards and election identity cards, did they have their names in voter lists, did they vote, what did they do for entertainment, did they consume any kind of narcotics, what was the first work that they did after coming to the region and why did they leave it, did they ever fall sick while driving the rickshaw, if yes then what did they do, how did they bear the cost of medication, did the rickshaw-owners cooperate during illness, if yes then how, did any kind of physical problem occur while driving the rickshaw, when did they feel tired while driving the rickshaw and how many hours did they rest during the night, and, was that sufficient?

Rickshaw-drivers were also asked whether they plied the rickshaws of their own or on rent, if on their own then how did they arrange for the money to buy it, and if it was on rent then did they have to give something as a jamanat (security money), if yes then in what form, for what duration did they get the rickshaw on rent, what was the daily rent, did they have to pay rent even for rest days, who was responsible for the maintenance of the rickshaw, what was the behaviour of the owner if the rick-

Table-2/ Estimated Number of Rickshaw-drivers

Name of the city	Estimated no.	Licenses issues
Alwar	7,000	2,087
Bhiwari	90	—
Ghaziabad	25,000	3,600
Loni	500	—
Modinagar	600	—
Muradnagar	1,000	—
Noida	7,000	—
Dadri	700	142
Meerut	35,000	12,270
Hapur	4,000	2,200
Bulandshahar	4,000	1,200
Khurja	2,000	105
Bahadurgarh	1,800	780
Faridabad	40,000	—
Palval	1,600	330
Hodal	150	—
Gurgaon	25,000	4,000
Sohna	250	84
Sonipat	3,000	1,500
Panipat	3,500	1,520
Rohtak	3,000	601
Rewari	4,000	218
Dharuhera	30	—
Delhi	3,00,000	73,000
Total	**4,69,220**	**1,03,641**

shaw got confiscated or it got lost, which zone did they get the rickshaw from, which zone did they ply it in and why didn't they buy their own rickshaw?

It was found from the rickshaw-drivers how long they had been plying the rickshaw, why did they choose the profession of rickshaw-driving, did anybody else in the family also ply the rickshaw, did they do some other work as well apart from plying the rickshaw—if yes then what, at what time did they ply the rickshaw and how many days in a week, what were their daily earnings, how much did they save daily and monthly, where did they keep their savings, what did they do with their savings, during which season did they earn more, did they send money back home from the savings, if yes then how much per month, had they ever borrowed money, if yes then why, from whom, how much and at what interest rate, for how many months in a year did they ply the rickshaw, why did people give precedence to the rickshaw over buses and cars, which people use rickshaws more frequently, did they have a fixed clientele and how much did they earn from it, what were the benefits of such clientele, had they ever carried anybody without money, did they eat two full meals? What were the minimum and maximum customer rents?

About licensing, rickshaw-drivers were asked whether they had licenses, if not, then why didn't they get it made, did they have the rickshaw pass, was their rickshaw ever impounded, if yes then what did they do to get it released, what problems did they confront while getting the rickshaw pass. What grievances did they have against the Municipal Corporation or the authorities, did they ever go to the Municipal Corporation with grievances, if yes then what was the result, did the traffic police or police impound their rickshaws, if yes then why, had the traffic police imposed restrictions on the streets, what was their opinion about the accusation that traffic jams occurred due to rickshaws, what did they have to say about the opinion of the government that rickshaw plying should be banned, did they feel that there should be a separate lane for rickshaws, a separate parking stand like the taxis and buses, how much fees did they have to pay to get the rickshaw passed, what was their opinion about the license fees, how much fine did they have to pay in case of a 'challan', did they have any information about the rickshaw drivers union, was there any need for such an organisation, was there any possibility of reforms in the present rickshaws?

In the 64 questions asked from the rickshaw-owners the details about their age, caste, religion, educational and marital status were found and then information was sought about their original place, what was their traditional family occupation, what was the reason for coming to the region, did they stay alone in the region or with their families, did they send some savings back home and how much, did their wives go to work and did their children go to school?

Rickshaw-owners were also asked about how long they had been renting out their rickshaws, why did they choose this profession, did they do some other work as well, did they ever ride the rickshaw themselves, if yes then when did they think of owning a rickshaw, what fees did they have to pay to get the rickshaw passed and what did they think about it, which papers were needed during the passing of the rickshaw, how many rickshaws had been passed by the corporation or the municipal council, didn't they feel that the rickshaws too should be registered throughout the year, did the license fee for the rickshaw need to be waived off, if yes then why, if no then why not, how much 'challan' fees was levied by the corporation or the council, did they have any information about the rickshaw-owners association, did they ever show their anger against the administration; what was the condition of the garage, if it was on government land did they pay rent for it, did they have any other garage in the city, did they get their rent on time, how much rent did they receive per rickshaw, how many rickshaws did they own, did they have any technical knowledge about rickshaws?

The owners were also asked whether people from the corporation or the council extracted money on a monthly basis from them, did they have to pay bribe to any departmental official, if yes then to whom, the corporation says that the rickshaw-owners exploit the pullers—what did they think about this, what incentives did they get from the government, should the rickshaw-business be given the status of a small industry, do the officials in charge of clearing the rickshaws have any technical knowledge, should there be a separate department for rickshaws, thelas and local vending, from time to time the municipal council destroys impounded rickshaws if they are not released by their owners—what do you think about it, what did they have to say about the allegation that rickshaws are responsible for traffic jams, does the traffic police or police impound vehicles or issue 'challans', did it happen to their rickshaws ever, then how did they get their rickshaw released, what grievances did they have against the corporation, does the Delhi traffic police prohibit rickshaws from plying on the roads, what is the main complaint against the traffic police and what do they do once they are 'challaned'?

To gauge the relationship between the owners and the pullers the owners were asked whether they could give security or residence certificate to the pullers so that they could get driving licenses, did they ask for security while renting out their rickshaws, if yes then of what type, if the puller falls sick then do they make any concession in the rent, shouldn't the rickshaw-drivers be given a rebate in rent on rest days, what do they do if the rickshaw-driver loses the rickshaw, what is the minimum and maximum age of their rickshaw-drivers, have they got a mechanic for repairs, where does the mechanic live, what salary does he receive, if there is no mechanic then who repairs the rickshaws?

Rickshaw-owners were also asked if they felt any need for a change in the design of the rickshaws, if yes then they were asked to give a suggestion, what did they think about the new rickshaw model and how did the society benefit from the rickshaw in their eyes?

Rickshaw-mechanics were asked 45 questions. After getting details about their caste, religion, educational and marital status, they were asked about their original place, what was their traditional family profession and since how long they were here, what was the reason behind their coming to the region, did they live alone or with their family, where did they live, do they send some money home after saving and how much, did the wife work and children go to school?

The mechanics were also asked what was the first work they did after reaching this region, when did they begin working as mechanics and how many hours daily and how many months in a year did they work, what did they do for entertainment, where did they get their medication from in the case of illness and what was the source of income during that period, do they do any other work apart from repairing rickshaws if yes then what, what kind of problems do they encounter while on work, have they taken any training for this work and does anyone else from the family do it too? The mechanics working in the garages were specially asked whether they needed license for this work, who brought them to the garage, when do they get their salary, do they get their weekly off or not, is their salary deducted in lieu of their holidays, does the owner help during illness, if yes then how, and do they have plans to open their own garages?

The mechanics working at their own places were asked how did they find that place, did they have to pay for it, if yes then to whom and how much, does the police evict them from this place, what is their daily earning, do they manage to save something daily, what do they do with their savings, who looks after the shop in their absence, what are the possibilities of changes in the rickshaw from the point of view of the drivers and customers, would they like to be trained for any positive change in the rickshaw?

Sixteen questions were asked from customers using rickshaws. After the identification of their age, class and gender, they were asked how often they used the rickshaw for transport, what was their destination, what did they think about the benefits of the rickshaw, what kind of vehicles were available for short distances in their eyes, should there be a separate lane for bicycles and rickshaws, which vehicles should be prohibited from entering the narrow lanes, should cycle-rickshaws be encouraged for lessening pollution, which vehicles are responsible for the traffic jams in the city, should the rickshaws be banned, are rickshaws a safe medium for transport, have you seen the new model of the rickshaw, have you ever fought with any rickshaw-driver over payment, did they have any memory of any specific rickshaw-driver, please give suggestions if you have any and do they know that the Delhi Municipal Corporation and Delhi traffic police destroy rickshaws after impounding them?

It becomes even more clear from the questions that the basic unit of this survey is indeed the rickshaw-driver, that rickshaw-driver who has been forced to come to the city having been evicted out from the village, he lives with the memories of the village, he has done various types of work after coming to the city and has realised in the end that the most respectful profession indeed is riding the rickshaw which made him taste freedom. Having been displaced and made a city-dweller forcibly, the rickshaw-wallah knows and understands that the chances of his economic progress are virtually non-existent, even then he is forced to live in the city and he is floating helplessly in the tide of modernisation and urbanisation unwittingly. It can be gauged from the results of the survey about the kind of possibilities that exist for this Asian citizen earning his livelihood through the tricycle, marginalised in this age of high-speed globalisation and what kind of contradictions does he represent on the ground of modernity.

Foreword

The Rickshaw Refuses to Go Away

The Struggle of the Co-traveller of Asian Modernity

Abhay Kumar Dubey

Dilli, meri Dilli!

—Writing on the back of a rickshaw parked at East Delhi's Anand Vihar Bus Terminal

Delhi is a cosmopolitan city… …In order to make Delhi a modern city equipped with a sophisticated transport system it has been thought better that not only the movement of cycle-rickshaw be restricted, but also other modes of transport like bullock-cart, tanga, thela etc should be banned as well.

—Deputy Commissioner of Police, Delhi in his statement given to the High Court

Globalisation and marginalisation are the counter-images of the same phenomenon, marginalisation being a necessary condition of globalisation while globalisation provides an existential framework in which millions are marginalised, felt unwanted and considered dispensable.

—Rajni Kothari: Under Globalisation : Will Nation-State Hold?

The last few days of August 2001 were something different for the lakhs of rickshaw-drivers in the National Capital Region (NCR). During those very days of struggle for a free and dignified life, they witnessed a ray of hope. They felt that even if late, they will finally be victorious. The importance of those days can be sensed through the details of two symbolic events. In the centre of one event was a 45 year old rickshaw-driver called Deepak Suri, and the second incident got linked to the country's Prime Minister Atal Bihari Vajpeyi. There was everything in these two episodes and in the narrative of their developments. It had the sad story of a cruel administration and the struggle of a poor man; it contained mutually conflicting meanings of old and new modernity; it had the Indian state posing as a mediator in the unrestricted flow of globalisation; it had a globalisation which cared two hoots for the autonomy of the Indian state and it also had the ruins of broken hopes. To a large extent one could guess through this narrative as to what was going to be the future of our cities' cosmopolitanism and also the direction in which our national life was going to turn in the coming times.

It so happened that on 21 August 2001, the Delhi Municipal Corporation confiscated Deepak Suri's rickshaw during routine raids made in the name of decongesting the city's streets. Deepak was asked for Rs. 400 as bribe, which he could not afford to pay. After failing in all his attempts to get the rickshaw released, he bought petrol worth Rs. 20 and threatened to immolate himself if his rickshaw was not returned. Deepak's only property was his old rickshaw, which he had acquired from another rickshaw-driver for Rs. 1200 a little more

Hand-pulled rickshaws on the roads of Simla in the last decades of twentieth century, which kept climbing the heights of this summer resort till the middle of century.

than a year ago. Legally Deepak should have had the license of the owner failing which his rickshaw could be confiscated. The reason for Deepak's trauma was that in case he was not able to get his rickshaw released, he would become completely bereft of his only source of livelihood. The administration could completely dismantle his rickshaw and sell it as junk.

On the third day of the confiscation of Deepak's rickshaw, i.e. on 23 August, a letter was sent from the PM's office to the Lieutenant Governor of Delhi, which contained a policy-related suggestion apart from the Prime Minister's letter. The PM had written to the Lieutenant Governor Vijay Kapoor emphasising that the restricted policy of giving licenses to the vendors and rickshaw-drivers should be changed. Their terrorisation due to restricted licensing system should be stopped. Vending and rickshaw driving should be given the status of a legitimate profession so that their poverty is reduced and these people could be included in the formal structure of the economy. The PM was especially worried about the fact that almost Rs. 50 crore

Most people agree about the existence of at least 3 lakh rickshaws. In this sense, the PM's letter could influence the lives of at least 15-20 lakh people.

bribe is extracted every month from the rickshaw-drivers and vendors of Delhi.

There were many things behind this concern of the Prime Minister. He was perhaps the first PM after Jawaharlal Nehru who had paid attention to the problems of rickshaw-wallahs. Atalji had travelled many times on rickshaw during his political life. He, as the leader of opposition, had even given a speech in a meet of rickshaw-drivers in the 1980s. It could be assumed, hence, that he would be somewhat aware of the movement of the rickshaw-drivers. Even this could be understood that the PM must be having some inkling of the equation between new economic reforms, the process of globalisation, urban transport and the poor rickshaw-drivers.

If we believe the data given by the Delhi's Traffic Police Commissioner Maxwell Pereira, the city has almost 10 lakh (one million) rickshaw-drivers. In reality, this is an exaggerated figure given with the purpose of banning rickshaws in the city. Despite this, most people agree about the existence of at least 3 lakh rickshaws. Hence, there should be at least as many rickshaw-drivers. This data will have to include almost 10,000 rickshaw mechanics, several thousand contractors i.e. rickshaw owners and thousands of people earning their livelihood through the spare part industry for rickshaws. Each person associated with the profession of the rickshaw looks after each family of at least 4-5 people. In this sense, the PM's letter could influence the lives of at least 15-20 lakh people.

The latest census tells us that by 2001, the total population of NCR had reached 13,782,976. A leader like Vajpeyi with such a popular image couldn't have neglected the political importance of

The hand-pulled rickshaw in the famous timber market of Simla in the dying years of the nineteenth century.

lakhs of people. On the other hand, as a PM, he had to ensure that the anti-poor tag of the new economic policy was also removed. If we look carefully at the relationship between the reduction in corruption and the success of economic reforms as defined by the former vigilance commissioner Narhari Vitthal then it looked as if the moment rickshaw-wallahs would move to the formal sector from the informal sector and the changes would be brought into the licensing method, effective stoppage would be enforced against the corruption at the lower level.

Needless to say that there was no direct causal relation between the letter of the Prime Minister and the threat of self-immolation given by Deepak. The struggle of life or death undertaken by the poor rickshaw-driver was going on separately and the PM, impressed with the initiatives taken by the organisations on behalf of the rickshaw-drivers, was taking his

Modernity itself had given birth to the rickshaw at one point of time. It was modernity, which used the rickshaw in order to extricate itself from various kinds of hurdles and it was modernity in its new editions, which became hell bent upon destroying the rickshaw.

own steps. How did Deepak manage to escape the fate of immolation and how did he manage to get back his rickshaw, is another story. What happened to the initiative taken by the PM; what was its inside story; did it reflect an honest wish to bring rickshaw-drivers into the mainstream of economic reforms and how did the administration manage to sabotage it—these are separate questions. A history of an umbilical relation exists between the rickshaw and modernity, which resides in the vast expanse separating these two stories placed at two distinct ends. Exploring this history makes one discover that present day's globalised modernity considers the rickshaw as a thing of the past and something completely unnecessary for the metropolitan cosmopolitanism and yet this rickshaw is basically a product of modernity itself and especially has been a co-traveller with the progress of Asian modernity. Added to this is the question that if Asian modernity doesn't need to necessarily restructure itself in accordance with the globalised structure laid down by the Euro-centric modernity, then can the rickshaw of Deepak Suri and others poor like him become a symbol of a small post-modern rebellion against the grand narrative of globalisation in the Asian context?

The rickshaw refuses to die

The reason for this kind of hope from the rickshaw is not only historical but contemporary as well. One doesn't need to take recourse to any great intellectual exercise to prove this claim. Facts are themselves proof of the truth. As we delve in the history of the rickshaw, we realise the peculiar existence of the rickshaw in the

Rickshaw pulled by Jhampanies was a major mode of commuting in the middle of the century Simla.

Asian context. We see that modernity itself had given birth to the rickshaw at one point of time. It was modernity, which used the rickshaw in order to extricate itself from various kinds of hurdles and it was modernity in its new editions, which became hell bent upon destroying the rickshaw. Yet, at the same time, we see that despite several attacks made by the different forms of modernity on the existence of this transport run on the human energy, it could not be done away with.

When the rickshaw was 'invented' in 1870 in Japan as 'Jinrikisha' (rickshaw driven by humans), nobody had estimated that it would prove to be the first step of the Japanese techno-industrial revolution which would gradually grow up to the level of DVD player and microwave oven. This first model of the techno-industrial modernity contained all the positive aspects of technological revolution. We know that only those inventions survive in the world of industrial technology of which the profits exceed their costs. Rickshaw can be considered as the first step of this revolution because since its birth it retains a standard of extremely profitable ratio between little investment and

The crisis of fuel during the Second World War had threatened to bring the traffic of the Asian cities to a halt. If the rickshaw had not been around, perhaps the urban system would have plunged into chaos.

a surplus, which is many times more. The rickshaw looks more attractive specially when seen in the Asian context, as the development of the huge, densely populated Asian cities would have been impossible without it. If life means to go on covering distances, the airplane cannot beat the rickshaw even today. The Jinrikisha, which was made in Japan, is still competing in terms of human utility with other transport produced by modernity.

The rickshaw proved its utility right after its invention. It spread fast all over Asia. Rickshaws became visible on the urban landscape of Japan, China, South-east Asia as well as the Indian subcontinent. Initially as private transport but very soon as public transport, the rickshaw was accepted by the Asian urban civilisation. It can be said that if there was something shared in the urban life of Asia, it was indeed the rickshaw. One and a half lakh rickshaws had begun to ply within ten years of its invention in Japan. Even emperor Meiji, famous for his economic reforms, rode around in a rickshaw in capital Tokyo. The present day's well-off Japan could progress due to the economic reforms undertaken by the very emperor Meiji, who not only established heavy industries with government investment, but also by setting personal example, got the rickshaw legitimacy in the Japanese society. By the time the 19th century ended, the rickshaw had become popular in Indo-china, Malaya and Burma. It reached Kolkata and Dhaka in the 1930s. It had begun to run on the streets of Delhi before independence. With the progress in industrial technology, cycle-rickshaw replaced the hand-driven rickshaw. Less human labour was needed to drive this while keeping its fast

The Sage of
RICKSHAW

61

की पुस्तकों पर 25% छूट दी जायगी। एफ.आ.आर.

6 / 011-23273167/23275710 पर संपर्क कर सकते

Gandhi heading towards the viceregal lodge in a hand-pulled rickshaw during the historical Simla conference.

pace. In the 1940s, cycle-rickshaws entered Delhi replacing the hand-rickshaws.

The contribution of the rickshaw in the development of modernity cannot be overestimated. In fact, modernity has used the rickshaw to get out of its troubles. The crisis of fuel during the Second World War had threatened to bring traffic in Asian cities to a halt. If the rickshaw had not been around, perhaps the urban system would have plunged into chaos. No fuel was needed for this vehicle. Initially it was thought that rickshaws were useful only for short distances but the period of fuel crisis proved that rickshaws could take their passengers to far off places provided the passenger had time and patience.

The moment the second Great War ended, the reconstruction of the destroyed cities began under the Marshall Plan and western editions of modernity began to overtake Asian forms. Europe and USA did not need the rickshaw. Local

Even in today's jet age, rickshaw, while ignoring the legal or illegal bans and oppressions, continues to serve the Asian roads.

trains, trams and buses had developed over there even before the rickshaw had been invented. Western societies had attained a certain level of prosperity due to the industrial revolution and colonial exploitation. There was no place for low earning rickshaw-drivers. American society, in fact, was gradually moving towards a stage where each individual could own a car. Western modernity saw the presence of rickshaws in Asian cities with distaste and in no time all kinds of discourses began against the rickshaw. It was alleged that rickshaws slow down traffic in cities and become the principal factor responsible for traffic jams. It was also said that rickshaws encourage illiterate and village bumpkins in the countryside to come to the cities which destabilises the balance between the city and the country. It brings unwanted pressure on the cities, which leads to the curtailment of public utilities, and islands of dirt and poverty begin to surface. Such allegations, which were articulated during the decades of 1940s and 1950s for the first time, are being repeated even today. Despite it being the product of European urban imaginaries, even the Asian ruling elite began to imbibe this discourse either due to a colonial mentality or under the influence of European glamour. Thus began a dichotomy out of which a growing distance from the rickshaw was clearly discernible. But eventually it was only a dichotomy; hence Asian cities could not deny the usefulness of rickshaws despite their administrators' distaste for it. Then taxis came on the scene; so did scooters, autos, buses, trams, local trains, metros—they all came and yet every time it was felt that it was impossible to do away with the rickshaw. Even in today's jet age, the rickshaw, irrespective of legal or ille-

Nehru heading towards the viceregal lodge in a hand-pulled rickshaw during the historical Simla conference.

gal bans and oppressions, continues to serve Asian roads.

Be it a capitalist or a socialist system, modern development has been unable to root out poverty and unemployment in the third world. Rickshaw-drivers, everywhere, are those poor labourers who have been displaced from the villages due to modern development. Fighting alone with the help of their rickshaws in the cities, these migrants serve and send the money to villages for the upkeep of their families. In this way, the rickshaw manages to create conditions so that the victims of modernity are not completely sidelined. Even if through illegitimate means, it brings them back within the orbit of modernity. In this way, the social base of the legitimacy of modernity has expanded, and it just about manages to go beyond merely being a slave to the rich and resourceful. If this is not a service to modernity, then what else is?

Despite all this, the western forms of modernity have given

'City of Joy' based on the life of Kolkata, has estimated that one lakh rickshaw-drivers carry 10 lakh passengers in one day in the city. In total, they cover so much of distance together that can't be covered jointly by the Boeings and Airbuses of the two airlines of India.

the rickshaw a raw deal. The westernisation of Japanese cities and the history of ill Treatment of the rickshaws can be seen going parallel to each other. Tokyo's administration has been obsessed with the issue of banning rickshaws for the last 50 years. The communist modernity of China banned rickshaws as symbols of exploitation immediately after the revolution and rickshaws began to disappear from the streets of Beijing and Shanghai since the last years of the 1950s. They escaped becoming almost extinct during the Cultural Revolution. Beijing administration's wrath fell on the rickshaws in 1972 during the visit of American President Richard Nixon. Nixon was not used to seeing rickshaws on the streets of a city. The same communist attitude could be witnessed in India when in 1996, Shubhash Chakraborty, a minister in the West Bengal government, announced that rickshaws would be completely banned on the streets of Kolkata. Even the governments of Thailand and Singapore tried to restrict or finish the rickshaws but remained unsuccessful.

Rickshaws returned to China in the 1980s. Beijing is generally known for its citizens with long faces, but its rickshaw-drivers are not of that kind. They look happier and more positive compared to the common citizens. Neither could the West Bengal government of the Marxist Communist Party destroy the rickshaw. Dominique Lapierre, the author of the famous novel 'City of Joy' based on life in Kolkata, has estimated that 1 lakh rickshaw-drivers carry 10 lakh passengers in one day in the city. In total, they cover so much of the distance together that can't be covered jointly by the Boeings and Airbuses of the two airlines of India. It has to be kept in mind that Kolkata is one such city in the world, which has both hand-pulled and cycle-rickshaws. Also, Dhaka, the capital of Bangladesh, cannot do without the rickshaw. As far as the cycle-rickshaw or the new edition of the rickshaw is concerned, one cannot find a better example than Dhaka in the Asian context of its usefulness. One out of three Taka spent on urban transport goes to the account of rickshaw in this city, which boasts of lakhs of rickshaws. The rickshaws of Dhaka are the most colourful and they sport many pictures on their backs, something that has led to several cultural research projects.

Sarojini Naidu in a hand-pulled rickshaw going for the historical Simla summit in 1939.

Needless to say that this predicament of modernity vis-à-vis the rickshaw has created a psychological problem for the citizens trapped in the ideas of westernisation. Those believing in capitalism see the rickshaw as symbol of backwardness, while those trained under socialist ideology consider the rickshaw as a symbol of exploitation. People travel in rickshaws under compulsion but with a sense of regret. For them it is an inevitable evil, like a spot on urban glamour. Socialist modernity is not in favour of depriving anybody of his livelihood but

Rickshaw driving is directly linked to 'right to life', 'right to earn livelihood' and 'right to work' in the Indian context. Rickshaw is a pollution free vehicle in his eyes and the initiative to preserve it can lead to global effect.

even they don't have any option other than destruction of the rickshaw. The cultural expression of this mentality can be witnessed in literature. The rickshaw-driver is a subject of pity in the eyes of pro-people poets. The poet feels guilty while sitting in a rickshaw. When those professing 'human' treatment to the horse see that a human is carrying him like a horse, he either gets off the rickshaw and takes away the rickshaw-driver's livelihood or hurts the rickshaw-driver's dignity by giving him extra tip. The socialist mindset is not ready to treat the rickshaw as a labourer. It is used to seeing the labourers of the formal sector as the only bonafied members of the working class.

Socialist thought looks at labour in relation to production, and evaluates its quality and revolutionary potential accordingly. The labourer working in a factory of heavy machines is a proper proletarian in its eyes. It advocates for his admittance in the primary school of Marxism, i.e., organising in a union. Since the rickshaw-driver doesn't produce anything, and only manages to earn his livelihood through his machine driven on human energy, his struggle for everyday existence can't bring him the membership of that grade of industrial labour, which Marx held to be requisite for not only social but also individual liberation. In fact it is at this very juncture where the rickshaw can play an important role in bringing Marxist thinking on the plane of practice. Marxists acknowledge the third sector (service sector) of the economy and accordingly organise bank employees into unions. Rickshaws, too, can be taken as a source of providing transport service to urban society on a small scale. This scale is small yet the need for it has continued for over 125 years and doesn't

seem to be going away in the near or far off future. According to Rajendra Ravi, who has researched the political economy of rickshaw-driving, even the pro-people mindset is not ready to accept that the cycle-rickshaw can play an important role in the developing countries in providing means of livelihood to the poor, can add to transport facilities and safeguard the environmental balance. They are not ready to understand the proven utility of the rickshaw in solving the problem of unemployment of weaker communities in countries like India, China, Bangladesh, Myanmar, Thailand, Indonesia, Korea, Hong Kong, Nepal, Philippines and Malayasia. If it is given encouragement in these countries then it can contribute significantly to attain the goal of just and enduring transport in urban life. Rajendra Ravi even goes on to claim that rickshaw-driving is directly linked to 'right to life', 'right to earn livelihood' and 'right to work' in the Indian context. Rickshaw is a pollution free vehicle in his eyes and the initiative to preserve it can lead to a global effect.

As the convenor of Lokayan and as a principal member of

Babu Rajendra Prasad heading towards the viceregal lodge in a hand-pulled rickshaw during the historical Simla conference.

The daily rent for a rickshaw is Rs. 25 after paying which Vinod still considers himself far better off than in the village. Compared to the oppressive life of the countryside, Delhi is indeed like a Dubai for him.

the Jan Parivahan Panchayat, Rajendra Ravi along with his friends has reached this conclusion after his study of the lives of rickshaw-drivers in NCR that in the times of extreme dependence on state or private capital, the rickshaw is one such unique medium through which even a semi-literate poor immigrant, unaware of life's complexities, can lead a free and dignified life despite remaining in an informal sector of labour. It is apparent that this life wouldn't have upward mobility of a middle class modernity. There is and will be a fixed limit to the income from the rickshaw but it will continue to save humans from unemployment, hunger, crime and dejection. On a global scale, the rickshaw could work as an 'antidote' to the terrible exploitation of energy resources. If we can save the rickshaw and get it a respectful position in the modern life, then there is every possibility that the earth might escape from a cataclysmic death in the event of an energy crisis. Jan Parivahan Panchayat is fighting this battle for the rickshaw in Delhi and surrounding towns. Though it is not the only one and there are other groups which are part of this struggle as well, Panchayat has a distinct viewpoint. The evidence for this was found when the PM wrote the letter to Delhi's Lieutenant Governor and other groups praised this initiative. Panchayat, on the contrary, called it a white-wash. Let's see what the Prime Minister's letter and his policy based initiative meant in the eyes of a common rickshaw-owner.

DILLI, MERI DILLI!

Vinod Yadav, a rickshaw-driver for the last five years in Sahibabad (which is adjacent to the urban areas of eastern Delhi) has written on the back of his rickshaw: 'Dilli, meri Dilli!' Is it possible that

10th fail Vinod or his rickshaw-owner had written this slogan after being influenced by the title of the serialised essay written by Maheshwar Dayal in the Hindi monthly 'Kadambini'? It was found upon asking the rickshaw-driver that only three days ago he had taken this three-wheeler on rent and he liked this 'exhortative' sentence. Why? Vinod got startled a bit by this question. Upon insisting, quite interestingly he said , 'Sahab, for us, this place is no less than Dubai.' As a free port in the middle-east, Dubai is a place where immigrant Indians go to earn money for a few days. Has Vinod come to Delhi to earn money? What will a rickshaw-driver earn and what will he manage to save? Yet, he dared to compare his migration to Delhi with the immigrant Indians of Dubai. The facts, which came out of a short conversation with Vinod, were like this: he had to work 24 hours in the fields of Bihar. To make things worse, he was also under constant threat of beating and abuse. Income was not even Rs. 10 daily. Out here, the rate for carrying one passenger from the Anand Vihar Bus Terminal to Vaishali Sector-V is Rs. 5 It takes only ten minutes to do this. Even if

Mohammad Ali Jinnah in a hand-pulled rickshaw going for the historical Simla summit in 1939.

It is almost like some inevitable law of history being played out—a law before which all the talk of equity and justice, or the old-fashioned notions of compassion and pity, appear meaningless and, of necessity, provoke so much cynicism.

one pedalled the rickshaw for the entire day with intermittent gaps of rest, it is still easy to earn between Rs. 50 to Rs.75. The daily rent for a rickshaw is Rs. 25 after paying which Vinod still considers himself far better off than in the village. Compared to the oppressive life in the countryside, Delhi is indeed like a Dubai for him.

It is evident that Vinod has not begun to consider himself 'unwanted and expendable' so far. In his own view, he is not incompetent, unsuitable and disabled on the scale of need. He has sought refuge in the city in the context of rapidly changing India of the the 21st century. Yet he doesn't know that the only thread between urban modernity and his pre-modern village, his rickshaw, has been declared un-modern by the powers that be of the city. Any time they can decide against him. The administration can impound his rickshaw in order to make the cosmopolitan modernity of Delhi at par with other big cities of the world. What will Vinod do then? Will he go back to drown his life in the feudal labour relations of the countryside? Or, will he somehow acquire another rickshaw and by carrying passengers on a somewhat 'secure' route, will try once again to make Delhi his own?

The metaphors mentioned above exist in Vinod's life either in a positive or in a negative form. Delhi belongs to him. It is his hope. Delhi for him is no less than Dubai. But whether he knows it or not, his existence in Delhi is dependent on the new definition of urban modernity. And this new definition of urban modernity comes out of the process of globalisation, which, in a few days will throw him off to the margins permanently. Rickshaw-driver Vinod is part of that society which is a victim of marginalisation.

According to Rajni Kothari :

> *... While also excluding from the global arena a whole variety of communities and cultures and literally billions of people: women and children, old people as well as the new generation of the young, the tribal, the forest dwellers, the landless and bonded labour in the rural peripheries and migrant labour in urban slums, the poor and discriminated sections everywhere... And as the fittest survive, those not considered 'fit' and 'meritorious' and 'deserving' must of necessity be considered dispensable. It is almost like some inevitable law of history being played out—a law before which all the talk of equity and justice, or the old-fashioned notions of compassion and pity, appear meaningless and, of necessity, provoke so much cynicism. This cynicism in turn lends weight and merit to the growing attitude among so many of disdain and contempt for the lowly, embarrassment at the presence of so many poor and destitute, unemployed and unemployable, found in whirlpools of debt—squalor and disease—and of*

Sikh leader Master Tara Singh in a hand-pulled rickshaw going for the historical Simla summit in 1939.

The PM's initiative doesn't show interest in simplifying the registration process for the rickshaw. Second, the rule is to issue only one license per person right now. This makes per person more than one rickshaw illegal.

crime. Such an attitude is not some bizarre or irrational psychic state. It is the net result of growing polarization between a minority backed by massive resources, power and the capacity to mislead and condition people's psyches, and a vast majority that is economically weak, socially divided and politically pushed to the wall but as yet unable to struggle together for evolving a common strategy to deal with the challenge posed by such a polarization.

The Place of Rickshaw in the Dream of a Global Delhi

Rajendra Ravi would perhaps be in complete agreement with this inter-relationship between globalisation and marginalisation. But even those social activists, who look at the process of globalisation positively, are forced to regard it with suspicion in the context of rickshaw-drivers. They conjure up a situation but can't sustain their imagination. In fact the system doesn't allow them even the luxury of armchair egalitarianism. One can cite the example of intellectual-activist Madhu Kishwar in this context who has been fighting for the interests of rickshaw-drivers in her journal 'Manushi'. She began her essay with a splendid imagination where she dared to enforce the rules and regulations meant for the rickshaw-drivers in the present system over the car and scooter owners:

One fine morning, the Delhi government suddenly declares that no more than 50,000 cars and scooters will be allowed in the entire territory of our capital city, without ensuring an effective public transport system to make up for private vehicles. It also

lays down that the ability to buy a car does not entitle you to own it. People have to have special government permits to own a car or scooter. Also that no family can get a license for more than one vehicle. Imagine further, that the government enacts a law stipulating that the person who is issued such a permit to own a car, a scooter, a bus or a truck has to drive that vehicle himself. If he allows someone else to drive it, the vehicle is liable to be forcibly seized by the Municipal Corporation and sold as junk, after being hammered to pulp. The corporation further legislates that in order to check the number of illegal vehicles, or those without permits on Delhi roads, the corporation employees and police have the right to carry out routine raids, stop any and every car/scooter driver and impound his vehicle, irrespective of whether he/she is able to produce his/her license or not. It then empowers itself to confiscate and destroy at random, as many cars as and when it pleases under the pretext of facilitating smooth flow of traffic.

And that in order to save this seized vehicle from being destroyed, the owner license has to prove within 15 days of seizure, that he himself was driving the seized vehicle. That even if there is clear evidence that the seizure was mala fide and that the municipal or traffic police inspector had confiscated several duly licensed vehicles simply to extract bribes, the owners of seized cars still have to pay a minimum fine of Rs. 40,000 each, or 10 to 20 per cent of the cost of their cars to get their respective vehicles released. That in addition, the owner licensee of the car has to pay Rs. 1,000 per day as store charges for the number of days that his vehicle remains confiscated.

If you want to turn this impossible dream of Madhu Kishwar into reality then replace the car and the scooter with the rickshaw. You will realise that this is what is happening in Delhi. Madhu Kishwar raises the question that when such a scenario can not be imagined about cars and scooters even in a dicta-

With a rate of Rs. 20 a day, a rickshaw driver has to pay Rs. 600 per month for rent. A new rickshaw comes for 3-4,000 rupees while an old one can be had in about twelve to fifteen hundred rupees.

torship or Fascist rule, then why are such restrictions brought against the rickshaws in the largest democracy of the world running under a liberalised system? The answer to Madhu's question can be found in the explanation entered to the High Court by T.N. Mohan, Deputy Commissioner of Delhi Police. One witnesses the commitment to make Delhi succeed on the global western criteria. And there is no place for the rickshaw in this global Delhi, which has been serving its citizens since even before independence.

Madhu Kishwar believes that the agenda of the new economic policy can be made pro-people. Hence she was hopeful that the PM's policy based initiative would bring a new ray of hope for the rickshaw-drivers. But she saw with dismay that the municipal officials are sabotaging the PM's attempts while colluding with the police and the administration. The oppression against the rickshaw-drivers increased on the contrary after the Prime Minister's letter. The frequency of raids and seizures increased, with greater strictness, municipal inspectors and the police began to prove that they couldn't be stopped.

According to Kishwar had the directions of the PMO been followed, the metropolis could have been divided into green, yellow and red zones. Rickshaws would have been given free access to the green zone; they could enter the yellow zone with a fee and the red zone could have been completely prohibited for them. But the traffic police by issuing a notification on 18 September 2001 banned the entry of rickshaws not only in the red zones but also in a large segment of the yellow zone between 8 in the morning and 10 in the night.

The question arises now that had the policy-based directions of the PM been fully accepted, the licensing system reformed and an alternative regulating method introduced, could those rickshaw-drivers, who consider Delhi to be their Dubai, have got a space in the global dreams of Delhi? Jan Parivahan Panchayat believes that even then it would have been impossible. Panchayat released a small document comparing the PM's alternative regulating method with the present system according to which:

☐ The Prime Minister has called for an end to the quantitative limit in the Alternative Regulatory System. While the Municipal Corporation of Delhi (MCD) and Delhi Cantonment Council issue licenses to rickshaw-drivers with a quantitative limit, the New Delhi Municipal Corporation (NDMC) retains complete ban on the entry of rickshaws in its areas. According to the rule, licenses exceeding 99, 000 cannot be issued in the MCD areas. MCD issues licenses to the owner and the driver, issues a license to a maximum of three people on one rickshaw in the event of joint ownership and to the driver, issues licenses to those drivers who are not rickshaw-drivers and also to the widows and disabled. Panchayat criticises Cantt. Council and MCD for releasing notification for the license only once a year. According to the record, these bodies have not been able to touch the maximum limit in terms of issuing the licenses till today. The main reason for this is their insistence on not issuing licenses throughout the year. All the rickshaw-drivers or owners are not able to obtain licenses in a fixed time-period. The PM's initiative doesn't show interest in simplifying the registration process for the rickshaw. Second, the rule is to issue only one license per person right now. This makes more than one rickshaw per person illegal. There is no provision to change this law in the PM's Alternative Regulatory System. Due to this very reason, rickshaw-owners can't have their business legalised, and fail to come into the mainstream of the economy. Most of the rickshaw-drivers are part-timers. Neither the present system nor the Alternative Regulation System thinks about them. The possibility of establishing something like a cooperative committee and making rickshaws available on a fair rent through this process has not been looked into. It

The character of already banned areas would not be altered and the areas which are available for the plying of the rickshaws would be divided into three zones out of which one will be designated as red zone. It simply means that the red zone will keep on increasing.

has to be kept in mind that with a rate of Rs. 20 a day, a rickshaw driver has to pay Rs. 600 per month for rent. A new rickshaw comes for Rs. 3-4,000 while an old one can be had for about Rs. 12 to Rs. 1500 This means that a rickshaw driver has to pay about 20 per cent of the price of a new rickshaw and about 50 per cent of the price of an old rickshaw as rent in a month alone.

□ The PM wants that Delhi should be divided into three zones of green, yellow and red. Effectiveness of this suggestion comes to naught when in reality the New Delhi Municipal Council decides not to issue any licenses. Apart from this, the bureaucrats of all the three city bodies have such absolute powers on the basis of which even the licensed rickshaws have been banned in a large section of the city. The traffic police has banned rickshaws on hundreds of roads, community complexes, markets and bridges. There is a provision in the rulebook of the corporation and cantonment that a rickshaw with a license from one zone will not be allowed in any other. PM's The Alternative Regulatory System doesn't look into these problems in the context of all the three city zones. The Alternative Regulatory System has been proposed only in the MCD areas. Government offices have been given rights to interpret the fixation of the boundaries. Many questions arise: How would the the red zone be defined? Will the rickshaws be gradually pushed out of Delhi in the name of the red zone? Is it not the case that non-inclusion of the Municipal Council in the Alternative Regulatory System is tantamount to accepting the ban imposed by it on the rickshaws? Cantonment Council and NDMC administer a large area of Delhi. How will the rickshaws be treated in these areas? Whenever the the Delhi traffic police wants, it bans rickshaws from passing through any area. What will be the criteria of such bans in the future? Will there be a renewed evaluation with a new perspective on the banned streets, bridges, community zones and markets under the Alternative Regulatory System or will the old ban continue? Similarly, there is a ban on rickshaws from going from one zone to another due to which they are often impounded. MCD issues licenses with different numbers in each zone. What will be the logical basis for this act? Will the numbers remain the same for the registration of rickshaws under the Alternative Regulatory System? The latter also doesn't explain that in the process of marking the boundaries for the zones which of the following will be given priority, motor vehicles or non-motorised vehicles?

□ As far as of cycle-rickshaws is concerned, there is a fee fixed for this along with which one has to submit domicile certificate compulsorily. The Alternative Regulatory System talks only of registration as an alternative to license. This registration will be made for a minimum possible fee on the basis of voter identity card, ration card, passport, a letter issued by the people's representative or a well-known citizen. This method doesn't dwell on the problem that for rickshaw-drivers to get their identity attested is most difficult. Documents proving their 'reliable identity' are outside their capacity. Most of the rickshaw-drivers are hardworking labourers having migrated from the countryside. It means that getting registration done would not be easy compared to acquiring a license. Also, registration is possible only in the Corporation zone and not in the Cantt. Council or municipal zone. The Alternative Regulatory System doesn't even mention the issue of registration of rickshaw-owners. Most of the rickshaw-owners have more than one rickshaw. In this sense, they have to indulge in illegal business because nobody can own more than one rickshaw. He has to acquire forged licenses under different names for each rickshaw. The Alternative Regulation Method doesn't look into the aspect of extricating rickshaw-owners from the vicious cycle of running their rickshaw illegally which is in fact a legitimate business.

□ Prime Minister's Alternative Regulatory System wants a change in the system of fixing boundaries. In reality, rickshaws can neither go from one zone of the corporation to another nor to the areas of the Cantt. Council or the Municipal Council. Second, the traffic police has divided the metropolis into several zones according to its own convenience. Due to this, the traffic police bar even those areas where the corporation allows the rickshaws to ply. A glance at the Alternative Regulatory System tells us that the character of already banned areas will not be altered and the areas which are available for plying rickshaws will be divided into three zones out of which one will be designated as the red zone. It simply means that the red zone will keep on increasing. Will those areas, now under complete control of the traffic police, be included in the renewed fixing of boundaries under the alternative regulation method? Or will they be kept out of the new system?

□ The Alternative Regulatory System mentions the role of social and non-governmental organisations in the context of

Dr. Ashraf Ali in a hand-pulled rickshaw going for the historical Simla summit in 1939.

rickshaw-drivers. Actually, the metropolitan bodies mouthing slogans of transparency and participation don't give any information of public importance despite written requests. The PM would have found evidence of this by now. Government departments refused to give any information regarding the steps taken for implementing the alternative regulation method leave alone taking any suggestions from non-governmental and social organisations.

Recently, Rajendra Ravi described the crisis of rickshaw-drivers and globalisation in these words:

> *... The government says one thing while something else happens in practice. Police atrocities on the poor rickshaw-wallahs have increased ever since the Prime Minister wrote that letter. Most of the streets have been barred for the rickshaw-drivers. Now they have the permission to ply the rickshaw in a very limited zone due to which they get few passengers. No passenger wants to hire a rickshaw regularly as it makes his or her cost of travel go high. For example, if somebody wants to go to Daryaganj from Yamuna-Pushta on a rickshaw, he or she will have to hire rickshaw twice because rickshaw are not allowed on the ring road. But in order to retain a passenger rickshaw-drivers violate this law very often. When traffic police catches them then it inserts iron-needle in the tube-tyres, sometimes holding them for hours and sometimes impounds their rickshaws in the local thana. The rickshaw-drivers lose out on their daily earning for the day. Similarly, street-vendors too face a lot of problems, as their movement has been restricted as well. Large iron gates have been placed at main entrances of many areas under the 'mutual security scheme'. This identified zone has been declared restricted for the vendors. They have been given space for organising haats (periodical markets) in such far-off areas that no customer will go there. Hence, the vendors refused to go there. Our policy makers don't even know that the customers of street vendors are different from those buying their wares from 'stationary*

haats'. Actually, the work of rickshaw driving and vending goes against the idea, which considers foreign capital as the key to progress. These are self-employed people which begin with small capital.

The Congress leader Subhadra Joshi organised the rickshaw-drivers and constituted their cooperative society. But MCD refused to give license to the members of the society. A movement was launched over this issue.

Jan Parivahan Panchayat shows through its criticisms that the Alternative Regulatory System of the Prime Minister is merely 'an attempt to cover the torn bed sheet with a new cover'. If the PM really wants to bring rickshaw-drivers into the mainstream of the new economic reform then he should have redefined the place of the rickshaw in the changed global perspective. It should have paid attention to the ownership right over the rickshaw, given it a priority in the transport planning and honoured rickshaws as an effective medium of environmental conservation and the livelihood of the poor.

Rickshaw in the Post-modern Imaginings

As an all-pervading phenomenon the meanings of globalisation can't be derived from those meta-narratives of the 19th and 20th centuries that had tried to mould humanity according to the whims and fancies of their imaginings. The rule of international financial capital drives the bulldozer of homogeneity more ruthlessly than those meta-narratives and does not leave any space for resistance. Actually, it not only tramples resistance but going beyond that subsumes it on the strength of its immense resources and power. The anti-statusquoist passions of endless radical theories and revolutionary blueprints have already been blunted through this 'lethal embrace' of globalisation. These theories and blueprints wanted to resist globalisation either through nationalist imaginings or through some class-based or some other liber-

tarian imaginings of a world revolution. They were, indeed, no more than projects of replacing globalisation with one of those meta-narratives that have been proven weak and ineffective. Globalisation didn't take a long time to defeat them. But, during the same time, a new rebellion was preparing to launch itself, which is named as 'the rebellion of small identities'. And these small identities don't invite you to go back to the 'caves of the past' at the expense of modern age. Actually, these identities are products of the early period of modernity in all senses. When the new age was constructing new theories and new claims to end old inequalities, most of these small identities were subsumed under meta-narratives promising to bring freedom. But the moment these meta-narratives were found to be hollow, these identities became free and sought independent claims. In the light of this perspective given by Aditya Nigam, it is clear that the rickshaw-driver is one such 'small identity' whose Asian character has been discussed above:

> *Today we witness the rebellion among innumerable small identities, which demand local autonomy and secession at times or get organised around caste, religion or gender at other times. Sometimes they raise the slogan of 'our village, our rule' or directly cross-examine the idea and practice of nationalism. This rebellion by keeping small identities at the core of their struggle has problematised the prevailing definitions of nation, class or citizenship in the last two decades. The fundamental questions of representation are once again being reopened today. No underprivileged section can think of its representation in abstract and flat categories established earlier. The mark of this period is that it has shown all these categories as merely attempts to retain the dominance of the hegemonic powers.*

Some conclusions can be drawn from this discourse. For example, small identities fighting for their place under the sun must consist of two enduring qualities. One, they should be distinct from the earlier established formal structures and second, they should have such an enduring resisting power which could

The corporation has destroyed about 60,000 rickshaws in the last 3 years though only 23,000 are listed in its records. They, in fact, want to make it extinct through constant torture. But the existence of this Asian child of early modernity continues.

retain their existence despite all attacks. We see that gender identity is once such identity, which refused to be tied to the formalities of the meta-narratives of nation and class. The patriarchal power of the market tried several times to destroy it but could not succeed. The labouring people of the informal sector survived despite their continuing exploitation and oppression. They neither got the help of capital nor did the modern technological development pay them any attention, nor the parties advocating revolution give them any respectable space in the ambit of working class by unionising them. The rickshaw is part of this same informal sector and 135 years of its history is witness to the fact that whenever attempts were made to restrict or destroy its existence, it kept surfacing time and again. This same relation between Delhi and the rickshaw is visible just like it is in other metropolises of Asia.

Hand-pulled rickshaws became popular in the cities of India during the of 1930s. Cycle-rickshaws came after independence. At that time, the Delhi government used to give licenses to 500 rickshaws. There was restriction on their plying from one zone to another. Rickshaw-drivers and owners were quite troubled over this. The Congress leader Subhadra Joshi organised the rickshaw-drivers and constituted their cooperative society. But MCD refused to give license to the members of the society. A movement was launched over this issue. The matter reached Prime Minister Jawaharlal Nehru. He ordered that 150 licenses should be issued to the members of the rickshaw cooperative society and the restriction from moving to one zone from another be lifted. The corporation acceded to the demand of issuing licenses but refused to lift the restrictions.

However, the experiment of the cooperative society attracted many people. Later, it became riven with dissentions due to political interference.

In 1960, special bylaws were passed for rickshaws in Delhi, which continued till 1975. The municipal commissioner gave licenses to 600 rickshaws under this. Later, 150 rickshaws from the Shahdara zone were added. The attempt to reduce the number of rickshaws proved futile as they kept increasing. The corporation was forced to formulate a new policy through a new survey in 1975. In 1976, a quota of 20,000 rickshaws was fixed. In 1993, it was increased to 50,000. The cycle-rickshaw operator union of the capital went to the Supreme Court against the arbitrary behaviour of the corporation. Police commissioner Mukund Upadhyay conceded in the court that though the corporation had issued licenses to 50,000 rickshaws, Delhi had over 4.5 lakh rickshaws plying at that moment. In December 1998, this quota reached up to 99,000. It is significant to note that the administration has outlined such a licensing process which never allows the rickshaws to reach maximum numbers. Till 2003, only 73,000 licenses had been issued. Hence, the rest of the rickshaws are technically illegal. The corporation has not released almost even one license for two year. The situation is such that if we assume that there are 3 lakh rickshaws in the capital, then only one out of 4 rickshaws in Delhi has got a license.

Legally one can't own more than one rickshaw. Only widows and handicapped are exceptions to this rule. Even they can't own more than five rickshaws. It is clear that if any person has 100 rickshaws then it is illegal. Such rickshaw-owners keep only 15-20 rickshaws with licenses. Even these licenses are obtained under bogus names through a bribe of Rs. 300 to 600. The officers of the corporation extract bribes as protection tax for the rest of the rickshaws. The license of ownership is issued only for three years but it has to be renewed every year. The fee for a new license is Rs. 50 and for renewal Rs. 25 but about Rs. 150-200 have to be paid as bribe. An illegal network goes on increasing through rules and laws in this way.

The practice of pedalling cycle in Europe and USA is increasing everyday. The use of rickshaws and cycles in China's capital Beijing has already been a subject of international discussion.

The reality is that the administration does not show practical interest in giving a license to any rickshaw as owner-driver on individual basis. It is difficult to extract bribes from different individuals while it can be done comfortably from rickshaw-owners (contractors). Corporation officers and policemen know which area has how many illegal rickshaws. The regular bribe-givers are given a 'pass word', which has to be written on the rickshaw so that nobody harasses them. For example, if 'Phoolchand' is seen written on a few rickshaws then it could be a code word. Bribe has to be given on licensed rickshaws as well though this is less than that for unlicensed ones. In 1998, the corporation made a cruel rule of impounding illegal rickshaws and selling them as junk by destroying them within 15 days. Even earlier rickshaws were confiscated but were released on a fine of Rs. 100 and a fine of Rs. 3 per day for standing within the precincts of the corporation. In 1998, this fine was increased upto Rs. 300 and the everyday fine is Rs. 25. It was also added that unlicensed rickshaws would not be released at any cost. This rule has increased the opportunity for bribery even more. Most of the rickshaws are impounded knowingly on Fridays, which makes it impossible to get them released before Tuesday. With fines of both kinds, almost Rs. 500 is lost on a rickshaw. If a rickshaw-wallah earns Rs. 100 a day then the loss on one rickshaw comes to about Rs. 800. Since December 2000, the Lieutenant Governor has allowed traffic police to impound rickshaws in order to lighten traffic on the roads. The important thing is that if a car is caught in a 'no entry' zone then it has to pay only Rs. 100 as fine but if a rickshaw is caught then it is impounded. If it is licensed then it has to pay at

least Rs. 325 for its release, if it is not then it has to pay a bribe between Rs. 200 to 400.

Apparently this description tells us that the rickshaw can become a natural part of the rebellion of small identities against globalisation and it indeed is. The rickshaw has to retain its existence illegally under the law all the time. It keeps increasing its numbers despite this. The urban elite advocating global modernity is ideologically against it. The corporation has destroyed about 60,000 rickshaws in the last three years though only 23,000 are listed in its records. They, in fact, want to make it extinct through constant torture. But the existence of this Asian child of early modernity continues.

The claim for environmental protection: the responsibility of traffic density

The issue of environment and ecology gains primacy automatically in the strategies of struggle against globalisation. Earlier, nobody could imagine that even rickshaws could be a medium of environmental protection. But ever since the automobile revolution happened in India, people looking for alternative modes of transport have begun to see the rickshaw as pollution-free urban transport. Clearly, this concept goes against the thinking of the advocates of the global capital. Delhi's air is more polluted than any other city of the world and it is not because of rickshaws but because of cars and scooters. Every year 2 lakh motorised vehicles are added to the traffic of the capital. More than the combined number of motorised vehicles in Kolkata, Bangalore, Chennai and Mumbai are running on Delhi streets.

Rickshaws are blamed for traffic jams but the cars are bigger culprits. It doesn't need much to understand this. A car travels fast by consuming petrol and diesel. Apart from being bigger than a rickshaw, it normally needs at least a space of 15 feet in the front and the back. And at least a five feet distance the left and the right. The moment this space is reduced, the speed of the car becomes slower than a rickshaw. A car can be used by a maximum of four or five people at one time though normally only one or two people are seen sitting inside it.

Comparatively, a rickshaw carries at least 60 people to their destinations in a day. Up to Rs. 20 are spent on an auto rickshaw to cover the distance of one kilometre while only Rs. 5 are spent on a rickshaw to cover the same distance. Along with this, rickshaws are a major medium of transporting children to schools in Asian cities, especially in Delhi. There is no better medium than the rickshaw to take housewives and old people to hospitals and markets placed at little distances. Rickshaws or carts do the job of transporting fruits, vegetables, wood, paper and construction material from the wholesale markets of Delhi to retail shops and other destinations.

Recently, Lokayan organised a unique exhibition in Hyderabad during the Asian Social Forum meet. It was a procession of rickshaw-drivers whose main slogan was 'protect the environment'. While talking to journalists, Rajendra Ravi claimed that,

Till now the rickshaw has been seen as an exploitative and insignificant activity, but the perception is changing now. Activist groups in developed and developing countries are leaving no stone unturned for raising awareness about the environmental aspects of the rickshaw. Work on its technical development is also going on. Researches are being undertaken to give the rickshaw a dignified human technique. It is being considered as helpful in poverty alleviation and in the protection of the environment. It is also gaining widespread acceptance as a medium of universally available mode of transport. Actually, even we need to evolve a traffic system according to local and native needs. Hence it is necessary that we look at the role of the rickshaw in new light.

Claims by Rajendra Ravi can be substantiated through many international examples. The practice of pedalling cycles in Europe and USA is increasing everyday. People have begun to prefer cycles not only for everyday travel but also to go to hilly areas for vacations. The cycle not only protects the ecology but riding it is also considered a good exercise. The use of rickshaws and cycles in China's capital Beijing has already been a subject of international discussion. Only recently,

Oxford has imported many rickshaws from Delhi. The number of cyclists is growing in the university campuses in Canada, Australia and Europe. Actually, the increase in the number of cycles can be seen as well as the increase in the number of rickshaws.

But Delhi is infested with the self-destructive propensity of the European urban architecture against this post-modern phenomenon. Attempts of all kind are being made to make it modern like New York and Frankfurt. Subways and flyovers are being constructed at huge costs. The reach of this modernity is limited to only well-off people. One rickshaw-driver says, 'What kind of modernity is this that no footpaths have been made on these giant flyovers nor separate lanes have been provided for cycle-rickshaws. The width of the road is being increased continuously but there is no scope for poor man's transport over this. There is a ban on rickshaws on most of these roads. The number of red zones are increasing continuously in the city.' The allegation of this rickshaw-driver is correct. There is a provision for a separate lane for slow vehicles in the Master Plan of Delhi, which the elite ruling the capital have forgotten.

As a representative of rickshaw-drivers, Rajendra Ravi asks that when the temperature of the earth is going upward and ecology is going to suffer from green house effect; environmental destruction is affecting those areas most where people exploit the nature least; when certain parts of India and Bangladesh have become susceptible to complete inundation by water; when there is a threat of many regions turning into deserts due to heat; when the rivers are drying; do the developing countries still need to follow those policies which the developed countries once followed but are now gradually giving up? The situation in many countries in Europe has reached the extent of creating car-less zones. Structural facilities are being provided to encourage cycling and walking in these countries. The importation of rickshaws from developing countries has begun. Can't developing countries like India play a pivotal role in this context by giving the rickshaw a respectable position on the basis of need and initiative? After all, our socio-economic conditions demand the protection and development of this sector.

In Asia, Singapore has begun to dissuade the use of cars. In India, the ownership of cars is being made as cheap as possible but in Singapore the individual ownership of cars has been made very expensive. The government of that city-state wants to protect its island from pollution by providing cheaper means of public transport. What does the Indian government want? What is its attitude and thinking? If Delhi is taken as a model, then an assessment can be made about the future of urban modernity in India. Studies done by Jan Parivahan Panchayat, Lokayan has attempted to find an answer to this question. 'The Cycle-rickshaw of NCR' is one such study.

Under the leadership of Rajendra Ravi, the team of Radheshyam Mangolpuri, Smita Snehi, Ishwar Joshi, Dhananjay Kumar Singh, Sanjeev Shashwati and Virendra Vidrohi studied the conditions of the lives of the rickshaw-drivers in NCRfor three to four years. These pro-people researchers have woven such a true story, which substantiates the post-modern reality in all its meanings and forms. If globalisation is a manifestation of extreme deformity of modernity then the saga of the rickshaw-drivers in NCR points towards those useful and pro-people aspects which are either trampled under the all-subsuming domination of international and financial capital or are under continuous decay for want of attention. The present book 'The Saga of Rickshaw/Identity, Struggle and Claims' is based on this study report.

Apart from Delhi, NCR also includes partially Haryana (Bahadurgarh, Gurgaon, Faridabad-Ballabgarh, Palwal, Hodal, Sonipat, Panipat, Rohtak, Rewari, Dharuhera and Sohna), Uttar Pradesh (Ghaziabad, Loni, Meerut, Noida Dadri, Modinagar, Muradnagar, Hapur, Bulandshahar and Khurja) and Rajasthan (Alwar and Bhiwari). The survey report has been prepared in the light of the history of the transport system and present problems of these areas. Readers will find concrete data, the halting progress of the technology of rickshaw-making and endless ironies and quiet hopes of freedom along with dignity in this analysis based on conversations with rickshaw-drivers, rickshaw-owners, rickshaw-mechanics, rickshaw-makers and rickshaw-passengers. The report actually emerges out as a long human document that has endless stories ingrained within it.

To avoid repetition and monotony, this report has been reorganised as a narrative of different aspects of the lives of rickshaw-drivers. It has been divided into three parts. The first part is titled 'City, Poverty and Labour' in which the issues of labour, freedom and dignity in the informal sector have been explored alongwith interaction between rural and urban poverty. The second part tells the story of 'Law, Identity and Struggle'. And the third part 'The Claims of Rickshaw' formulates their demand. I am hopeful that the story of rickshaw-drivers in NCR will touch the soul of sensitive citizens and will provide a new arena of struggle to the concerned activist-thinkers. They would understand that the small identity of a rickshaw-driver can be counted in opposing the onslought of globalisation.

□□□

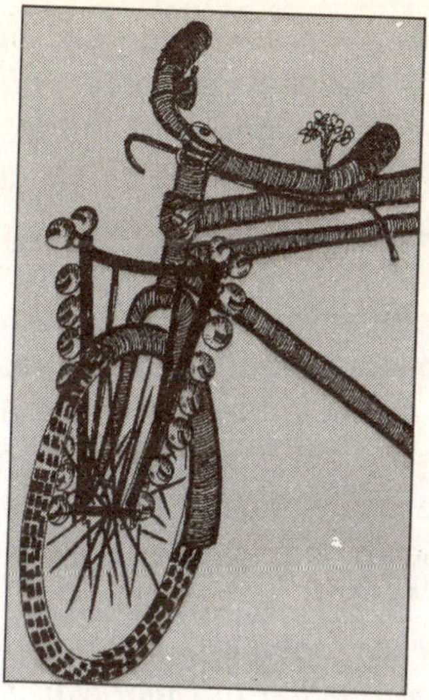

ONE

City, Poverty and Labour

Rickshaw and the Lives Dependent on It

It sounds egalitarianism, though,
That we take our horse for a human, too,
When it really happens to be a human;
Filled with guilt we get off the rickshaw,
And regret why we should have hit at his job,
And in a pity dole out a tip.
In all three instances, we are the load, and he the carrier.
Only as they haggle over the freight, the two level off.
Come, O the 21st-century engineer
Let us invent a cyle-rickshaw
That seats both the rider and the horse
Side by side with ease.
But you may ask, what for?
Well, the horse then need not turn his head and ask,
In case he disagrees.

—Raghuveer Sahay

If somebody were asked to paint an average rickshaw-driver of the National Capital Region (NCR), what kind of lines would emerge on paper? Clearly, it will be of a poor labourer from a rural background. But, then will that picture also have a colour of modernity or will it merely have the hues of tradition? Or will this painting belong to a person who is also carrying the burden of his traditions along with his passengers in the modern sphere? Will there be expressions of hope on his face or will he be only in the grip of his labouring present? All these questions are extremely tough to answer, especially in the context of rickshaw-drivers. The picture of an average rickshaw-wallah which emerges out of a study of a sample of 3500 rickshaw-drivers in NCR, is something like this:

> *The colour darkened with the beatings of the extreme sub-tropical weather of Delhi (which makes it difficult to make out the colour at birth); age around 35 years; tattered and discoloured clothes smelling of sweat, slippers on the feet or barefeet; used to khaini or smoking biri; mostly Hindu by religion and belonging to middle caste, illiterate or educated up to fifth-sixth grade; sleeping on the footpaths or living collectively with other rickshaw-drivers in a slum or an unauthorised colony; going to the open fields for defecation; experience of farming once upon a time, wife and children in the village; attempt to save and send Rs.1000 to Rs. 500 to the village somehow; rented unlicensed rickshaw and monthly income of is at most Rs. 3500; no hopes of an increase in income or the betterment of the life-conditions though a vague feeling of freedom in driving the rickshaw; jest for life with a sense of sarcasm; the constant fear that anytime the police or the administration can impound and destroy his vehicle; satisfaction of having escaped from the grip of the feudal production relations of the village; entertaining himself by playing cards or by listening to the radio; neither any ration card nor any identity card, no name in the voters list; neither communists come to*

him nor the Jansanghis.

Needless to say that it is merely an average picture of a rickshaw-driver constructed through bold strokes. Rickshaw-drivers, entirely different from this sketch might be found. For example, most of the rickshaw-drivers of Alwar (a city in NCR) have their names in the voters' list because they are local residents and haven't come to drive rickshaws from some far-off place. Similarly, rickshaw-wallahs living in their own houses could be found too. There are rickshaw-drivers who get high on smack instead of biri or khaini. Rickshaw-drivers having gone back to their villages can be found too. Despite these differences, this average portrait of a rickshaw-driver tells that he is a person, who, having immigrated from the village to the city, will try his best not to go back.

The reason is that the city can give him what he can't get in the village. In lieu of little payment he labours hard to serve the city, yet the city hasn't given him the well-defined identity of a citizen so far. He is fated to live on the margins of urban society for want of a legal identity. The city does want to take his services but refuses to accept him. The question is why such a contradiction? What kind of utility does the city have of him and why doesn't it want to own him?

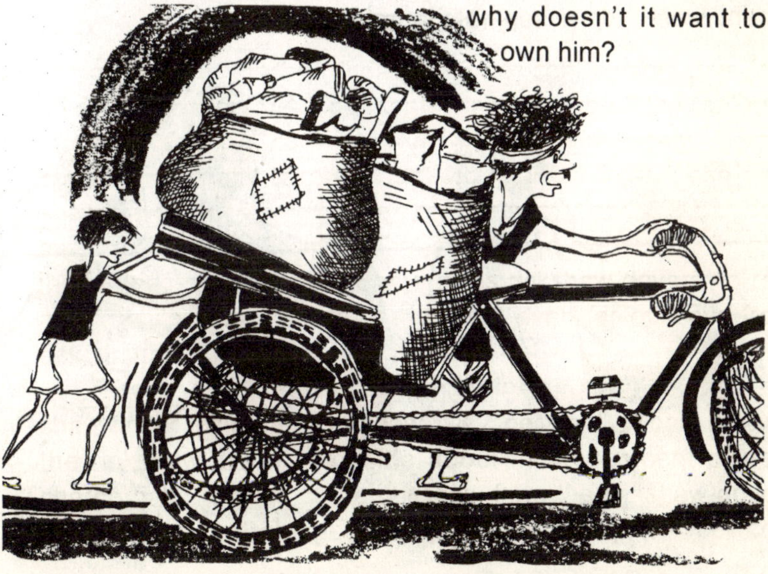

The rickshaw surviving on grounds of utility as against speed

At least 6 lakh people ride rickshaws in NCR and people numbering more than ten times travel by rickshaws. Rickshaws carry goods of small traders and take small children to schools. It is the most useful transport for sisters and daughters to travel home from bus stops. It is impossible to visit the haat-bazaar of the colony without the rickshaw. Along with the huge number of rickshaw-drivers and the people travelling on it, a small community of rickshaw-owners, rickshaw-mechanics and rickshaw-makers is also associated with this tricycle. Despite the incremental rise in the numbers of private scooters, cars, public buses, mini buses and suburban trains every day, this study of the people related to the rickshaw is enough to prove how essential it is for the transport of the largest urban region. When the citizens of the territory were asked whether rickshaws should be banned, 41.8 per cent people answered in the negative. Out of these, 87.4 per cent people considered the rickshaw to be a safe medium of transport and 97.2 per cent people thought that the rickshaw should be used as a effective tool in the battle to save the environment of the city, 93.1 per cent were for a separate lane for bicycles and

rickshaws.And 94.3 per cent of the people thought that the rickshaw is the most easily available transport for short distance travel. Apart from travelling to bus stations and railway stations, people travel on rickshaws to go to schools-colleges, markets and offices. More than 50 per cent rickshaws travellers prefer to use this tricycle running on human fuel. Compared to any other vehicle, per kilometre expense on commuting through the rickshaw is the least.

All kinds of up-market means of transport are coming on the street today. Their number and models are increasing everyday. Their speed too is increasing everyday. Yet they are not being able to beat the rickshaw. The number of rickshaws is increasing regularly. Their customers too are increasing. After all what is the reason behind the rickshaw's tenacity in front of all these challenges? Why do people travel in rickshaws despite buses and motor vehicles?

Rickshaw-drivers answer this question differently according to their respective experiences. 23 per cent rickshaw-drivers feel that people take rickshaws in order to avoid crowd. Rickshaws travel through even narrow by lanes and bring one to the doorsteps. 20.3 per cent and 30.5 per cent rickshaw-drivers consider these facts respectively to be important in favour

of the utility of the rickshaw. Three per cent rickshaw-drivers even say that since the rickshaw carries luggage too apart from people, hence its demand continues. Rickshaws are available everywhere, one can reach anywhere from anywhere in a hurry by it; a rickshaw-driver easily agrees to commute short distances, in such a case its rate is less as well—rickshaw-drivers consider these reasons behind the availability of commuters for rickshaws.

Who uses the rickshaws most frequently? Rickshaw-drivers answer this on the basis of the kind of people they carry in maximum numbers. Evidently, there will be considerable difference in the experience of different rickshaw-drivers. A few rickshaw-drivers (1.5 per cent) hold the elderly, some others (7.8 per cent) consider women, a few (1.1 per cent) hold students and a few others (3.4 per cent) hold people with luggage most frequent users of the rickshaw. But most of the rickshaw-drivers don't give importance to only one among these. According to them, all kinds of commuters use the rickshaw. People holding such a view is in higher percentage in all the sub-regions—Haryana (93.7 per cent), Uttar Pradesh (93.8 per cent), Rajasthan (86.2 per cent) and Delhi (51.5 per cent). The ques-

NCR's areas : Some Images around Rickshaw

The Hutment on the Footpath

A confiscated rickshaw store. On the footpath adjacent to the ring-road are three temporarily chulhas made out of piled on bricks. One has vegetables cooking on it, on the other are roties being prepared. The third chulha is idly wondering about the ways of the world. Something must have cooked on it at night. These thick chapaties are being rolled and cooked on tawas by men. Two of them are cooking, the rest are gossiping. The memory of the home keeps them warm

One of them loaded his chilam and puffed up thrice. They are all seated on a mat in the shade of a tree. All their belongings lie near-by—a tin box, some bags, some aluminum utensils, some blankets and odds. This group of seven or eight is that of rickshaw-drivers. They have homed in on this footpath. All of them have migrated from some vil-

lage in Shahjahanpur. Rickshaws they have taken on rent. They cook collectively and share the expenses among them. Jagdeesh says, 'Rooms in this area are costly, and we have chosen the footpath because we don't earn much. We have come all the way to raise money and if we are not in a position to send anything home—why the hell are we living here? '

Thirty feet away from this group is another group of 7–8 people. They don't have even a box. Some bags hanging on the branches and that's all. The fuel for the chulhas here are branches and twigs. Dheerendra says, 'This pardes is like a vanvas for us. If it starts raining we'll have to run around to collect things under some shade.'

Many of the rickshaw-drivers keep their bags hanging on the railing of a park. All day they pull rickshaws, gulp down something on a footpath dhaba and come straight to their bags to sleep. Nothing but some clothes are there in those bags. Shivdayal says, 'Now the owners don't bother to provide for a little space under the seat for the driver to throw his bag in.'

Two Rickshaws in South Delhi

Vasant Kunj Enclave. A new colony spread over the area of one sq. km. The only vehicles connecting this colony to the main road are two rickshaws. Social activist Rita Nahta, a resident of the same colony, informs us, 'One of these rickshaws has been provided to them by the colonizer of this colony and the other by the Resident Welfare Association. They don't have to pay the rent but the maintenance is theirs.' Another resident reports, 'The wages for plying up to the main road is Rs. 5 per adult and Rs. 2 per child.' Madhav and Ratan are the rickshaw-drivers. They are happy here. Every day they raise money to the tune of Rs. 50-60. In addition to this, 'we bring the colony-kids home from school. We drop them to their respective schools. This means a monthly income of Rs. 110 per child. Which helps us raise an additional income of Rs. 2500 to 2800.'

This could be treated as a good beginning!

Once Loni was on the Bank of the Yamuna

The story goes that the small town of Loni was developed around a fort by Raja Loonkaran. Spread all around the fort, now it almost shakes hands with Delhi. Arshad hails from Loni, 'Now the Yamuna has parted ways with Loni but that huge unshakable stone was once in the middle of the Yamuna. We called it "Hathi Ka Khoonta". This was raised, I guess, for anchoring the boats... Once someone tried building a private house against the rock but the rock pulled it down.'

'Another memorable thing here is the pond of Ranpa village, spread across 300 acres of land. It was once surrounded all over with a strong wall. Most of it stands dilapidated. People walked away with rocks... but one part of the wall is still intact. This gives the idea that once it must have been a large water body. Loni is spread up to the walls of the pond. The wall forms the foundation some of the houses,' says another man.

People from the older generation are hardly there to report, but in any case the history of modern Loni can't be traced beyond three or four decades!

Rohatak: Rickshaws Within and Buses Without

Rickshaws, cycles and auto-rickshaws ply in this township. Autos take passengers only on some of the main roads, and never charge less than Rs. 4 per person. This goes in favor of rickshaw-wallahs, and all over the city people naturally prefer taking rickshaws for short distances. Buffalo-carts and horse-carts are there for carrying goods from one end to the other. Bharat Singh Pawar, now 71, the editor of the local fortnightly, 'Bhola Insan' states, 'Rohtak is expanding fast. Villages like Sainipura, Kishanpura, Ajkadgarh, Sukhpura, Para etc. are part of the township now. The population now is something to the tune of 3 lakhs. This has naturally taken a toll on upon the transport system of the town. Earlier the roads were paved only with stone chips and to fight dirt, the municipality had to sprinkle water on them.

Till 1960 the town had only about 100-150 tongas running from the bus-stop to the Medical College and villages. Some tongas connected us to distant villages like Sanpala, Beri and Gohana. Most of the people traveled by foot because they were invariably short of money. Rickshaws came to Rohtak around 1955. (Moreover, going on foot was not considered sub-standard then). Those days there used to be a kerosene lamp hung on the front wheel of the rickshaw to fight darkness on roads. Around 1955-56 the tractors came. Buses never ply inside the town. Rohtak saw three-wheelers in the 1980s. They are popular these days.

Modinagar: The Making and Unmaking of the Town

Ramkishore Sharma (aged 65 years), a worker with the Khadi Gramaodyog Sangh lapses into memories, 'In 1933 this Modi family migrated from Patiala to Beghamabad. Their sugar mill soon moved into a cotton mill, lantern mill, vanaspati ghee mill and soap mill etc. This provided a definite employment base and added to the population of the township. Catering to the needs and demands of the employees, the Modies raised colonies and quarters, school, colleges, hospitals and temples too. Everything was Modified.' They had that penchant of social service in them. They looked for the right hands, trained them, but by 1980 they started folding up.

A garment vendor on a cycle, Ramkumar, who was born in Modi Nagar in 1968, recalls, 'This city progressed under Modies and got ruined because of them also After 1983 with every passing day financial condition of the city became worse as the Modies started folding up and closing down mills and many people came back on the roads again. Funds, bonuses, salaries came to a dead halt. Political leaders gave assurances, which in fact never materialised. Dejected migrant workers left the place and local workers kept waiting in their dwellings in the hope that one day they will get their dues. Now everybody has become uprooted. Some have migrated to bigger cities, some have survived as vendors and rickshaw-drivers! But this is survival at the basic level. This depopulated town has run out of resources. Due to a lack of fruitful employment the paying capacity of the people here is very low. Very few of them can afford to ride a rickshaw! Obviously, the income levels of rickshaw-drivers has come down considerably. People are gradually leaving this profession, and the number of rickshaws is decreasing. Few are still clinging on with no alternative in sight. Most of the shopkeepers sit with their shops open, eagerly waiting for a customer or two to buzz in.'

Hapur: Chaos on Roads

There are red lights on Ambedkar Chowk and Tahseel Chowk, but these lights are out of order! There is hardly

anyone for traffic control. People exercise their own survival instinct. Because the town is small, there are few instances of traffic jams, but an accident is always in the offing. There is no slot for parking. Vendors set up their shops on the footpath. This curtails the space on broad roads too. Pulling a rickshaw here keeps you on yours toes. Rickshaw-drivers generally avoid crowded roads. They don't mind taking a longer route. Railway gates are another great hurdle. They disrupts the traffic off and on. The golden way out is the forlorn road between the railway station and Malgodam. It is zigzag and broken but safe at least.

Alwar: His Vehicle and Yours Too

The town is known by three names: Ulwar, Alaur and Alwar. Maharaj Jai Singh gave the town a face-lift in the first two decades of the 20th century. He built many roads and gave it a Hindi name. During the reign of Maharaj Tej Singh, his Prime Minister Harvey modernised the town.

After independence the cities around the town filled up and new colonies came up. In the last few decades it was heavily industrialised and since then the town has been expanding. Rajasthan Housing Board and Development Trust are raising new colonies and the unauthorised colonies are an extra baggage. During the time of kings, the king and his retinue traveled on elephants and horses, and the common people had camels and ox-carts to ride on. Gradually the elephants and horses were replaced by motor cars and the camels and ox-carts by tongas. Around 1961 the rickshaw made a grand entry. But at that time the rates were so high that only the rich could afford it. With the passage of time it came closer to the common man, and today especially in the old city where the lanes are narrow, rickshaws are the only companions for the man on the street.

Meerut: The Best in the Rickshaw Body

Meerut's fame as a touch flows from the fact that in 1857 it was the springboard from which the first freedom movement was launched. It has district and commissioner's headquarter too. In terms of modern development, more than a 100 industrial units provide the base for employment. A strong work force survives on it. More than that, this town provides solid bodies to the rickshaws plying all over north

India—Punjab, Haryana, Rajasthan and Uttar Pradesh. Besides goods, scissors and ghazak, rickshaw bodies have earned a distinction for this old city of many gates. It seems that a wall at some point of time must have surrounded the city! What else could explain so many gate here—Dilli Gate, Burhana Gate and many others. There are a few other monuments of historical importance lying in deprecation with no maintenance. Nobody seems to take an interest in developing them as tourist spots. Three old libraries can be found in an extremely rundown condition. On railway road, a museum containing the exhibits of 1857 has yet to be thrown open for the public. Only last year a huge memorial was erected in these premises to celebrate the famous revolt.

Delhi: Smack is the Salt of Life

The over bridge in Yamuna Bazaar at 5 pm in the evening. Under the bridge a gang of poor dopies, enjoying their stuff of grass, smack and charas. Some of them are having drug injections too. A case of poor people addicted to the ways of the rich. Policemen come and hound them out with their

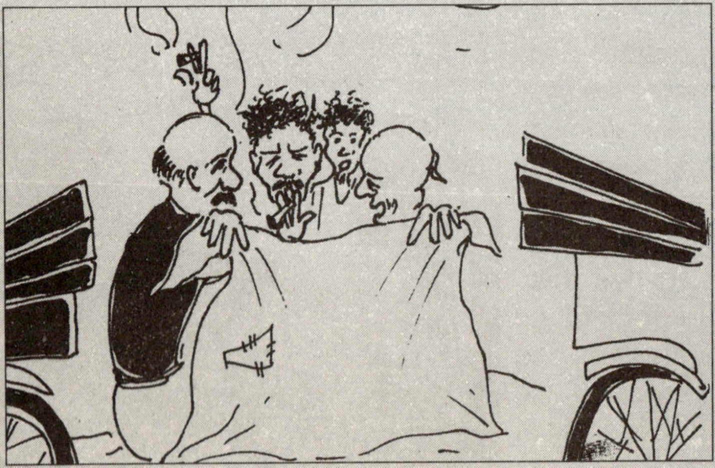

sticks. As a defensive ploy they spread out side-ways with their belongings. The moment the policemen go, they are back again, in groups with their stuff, because smack is the salt of life for them.

Behind the cover of a bed sheet three people are smoking smack, lighting a match repeatedly. On of them, Rajendra Chowdhary (46 years) repents, 'Babujee, it is so costly. It cost me my job too. I was a cook for years but smack threw me on the streets. Somehow I am surviving as a rickshaw-driver now.' But his fellow-dopies—Lal Bahadur (26) of Gorakhpur: says 'Today I had earned Rs. 100, but smoked them out. Now I have no money for food, but you know smack is more necessary.' The third dopey went away without saying anything, and in his place came Doonu Yadav (37) of Allahabad who admitted: "I drive a rickshaw, the day I don't get it on hire I push a thela. Some day I labour in a marriage party. Whatever I earn, I spend on food and dope. No saving at all.'

Doonu, educated till class six, wears clean clothes and sports a clean-shaven look. He says: 'All my friends are dopies, but we live cleanly. Whatever we earn, we spend on smack. We have one set of clothes each but we keep it clean. Every morning we wash it and get it ironed occasionally. We have one rickshaw between us, which we ply in shifts.

The owner charges Rs. 25 everyday. We share this too. We sleep in the park but hardly do I keep any money with me. Smack takes you to cloud nine, and once on cloud nine, one is totally oblivious of the immediate surroundings. I had bought a pair of Action shoes recently. They were lying next to me, and someone took than. Some people work in night shift. Got my point?'

tion is, isn't such a positive attitude towards any transport enough to make it a compulsory, respected and comparatively permanent part of urban transport? Delhi has trains, taxis, autos and buses. But the kind of deep relationship an ordinary life has with trains and buses is no less in the case of the rickshaw. Scholars the world over are unanimous in the view that the meaning of democratic administrative process amounts to giving primacy to everyday life the most. Any person with common sense can understand the utility of the rickshaw in everyday life. If the rickshaw is banned today, there will be an unbridgeable vacuum in urban life. But despite this common sense what is the reason due to which only 73,000 rickshaws have been issued licenses in the Delhi city zone and the rest all the rickshaws ply illegally? What is the reason due to which senior officials of Delhi police, in their submissions before the

Rickshaws in IIT

IIT is the only place in South Delhi where rickshaws ply—11 modern rickshaws prepared by IIT engineers.

One of the drivers, Suresh Kashyap reports, 'I was a daily-wager in this institution. For the last three years I have been pulling one of the four rickshaws plying on the campus. Then four more rickshaws were acquired. IIT doesn't charge any ren for these rickshaws but the maintenance is ours. There are no mechanics on the campus. Repair shops are all at Adhcheeni. The rate list is pasted there at the back of the rickshaw—the minimum that we can charge is Rs. 2 and maximum Rs. 8. Anybody can board us but we have to ply only within the campus. In summers the average of what we earn is Rs. 100 but in winter it goes down to Rs. 70. During the vacation it slumps down further to Rs. 40.'

areas of the city are not properly linked with buses. The answer to this mess is not only the broadening of roads and the building of overbridges. In fact, these measures are not

Rickshawdom at Yamuna Pushta

The working class, mostly immigrants from the various parts of the country, dwell on both the banks of the Yamuna, and it make for a different world altogether. The basti is thick on the other side, from this side of Pushta to the foot-lands of the Yamuna. Rain sweep away many hutments and summer burns down many in fires. Many of the rickshaw-drivers live here and there are around 50 rickshaw garages in the area. The nearby Yamuna Bazar area also has many garages. Easily it can be termed as a Rickshawnagari.

Shahdara North and Shahdara South are both beyond the Yamuna and there are many bridges across the two parts. Two of them are railway bridges. Recently a modernised toll-tax bridge has also come up. It connects Delhi and Noida. Three pontoon bridges come up for summer days to cater to the light vehicles. During the reign of Shahjahan a bridge of boats was raised near the old railway bridge. Those were the days when boats sailed in this river for the purpose of transportation. Twenty five—thirty boats sail in the Yamuna now a days. Farmers use it for transportation and some use it for collecting coconuts and clothes offered in the Yamuna.

court, consider the existence of rickshaws a threat to the modernity and global identity of Delhi? What is the reason for the apparent lack of interest in providing separate lanes to bicycles or rickshaws on the Delhi flyovers and rapid highways despite a mention in the master plan?

The answers to these questions can be found perhaps in the character of the city. NCR is a strange structure. Delhi is engaged in appropriating many urban, semi-urban and rural areas of Haryana, Rajasthan and Uttar Pradesh adjacent to it through this project. Formally this region has been constructed on paper but informally it has not acquired the form of a huge, naturally interrelated zone. The plan created by the National Capital Region Planning Board which became operational on 23 January 1989, aimed to make this area spread over 30,242 sq. km. into a model of urban development worth following. This region is a living example of how the geography of modernisation puts its foot forward through urbanisation and the units of village life get absorbed in it one after another. Villages and semi-urban areas become part of the cosmopolitanisation of a growing metropolis. For a short while, they retain their original names but very soon the existence of these villages in terms of their names, people and ambience disappears whose peasants' land would be appropriated by some authority or the government at random prices. For example, Patparganj turns into I.P. Extension and many areas of Sahibabad acquire sanskritised names like Vaishali, Koshambi or Vasundhara.

In this very process of obliteration of a history and the making of a present one, does the modern time proceed. Many

The Wasteful Train

Here in Delhi in addition to the 38 railway stations (New Delhi, Old Delhi, Sarai Rohilla and Hazrat Nizamuddin being the prominent ones), there is going to be a network of metro stations too. Avenues of education, employment, medical treatment and better business draw lots of people to Delhi, which is well connected with the other parts of the country. But, the city-railway service has not proved to be as useful as it is for cities like Mumbai.

There is a ring-train also. Travel on a ring from Nizamuddin to Nizamuddin takes one and a half hours, 27 railways stations fall on the way but because of the paucity of connecting buses and cycle stands, very few people utilise these. Instead of improving upon the existing infrastructure, the government has gone whole hog investing in Metro. The Metro Rail service will cover 34.5 km. of land under the surface, 53 km on the surface and 111 km thinking people consider this as progressive and forward looking but due to this ideological prejudice they don't see the interrelation between the city, poverty and labour under which the oppressed, weak and helpless forms of human life get constructed. Whether it is NCR or even a bigger region than that, the expanding city emerges as a refuge for displacement coming out of the womb of poverty in villages and the changing production relations. On this very land of expanding cities, class-relations are formed and new communities get constructed breaking out of the boundaries of caste, religion and older forms of the community. In the triangle of labour, poverty and city the mixed forms of rural and urban lives develop.

In the conflict of formality and informality the questions of human dignity and freedom as against the dignity of the elite begin to appear once again. The relationship between Delhi and the rickshaw-drivers is of a similar type. First, Delhi became the capital, then it became the National Capital Zone and now it is National Capital Region subsuming adjacent

above the surface. People are both curious and apprehensive, about the exorbitant tickets and limited routes.

Ex-secretary of Delhi government,Umesh Sehgal comments, 'The bureaucracy prides itself on building New Taj Mahals every now and then. These Taj Mahals may be beautiful but they do not serve any purpose: the ring-rail and the metro-rail are two burning examples.

Eighty crores were spent on the rail-ring during the Asiad and now in the list of white elephant figures the Metro Rail. How fruitful can the venture of connecting Nangloi to the ISBT and Delhi Univercity to Central Secretariat might be? Wrong target points both for the villagers and the students. So much has been spent to serve the interest of just the 5 per cent of the passengers. Providing additional buses would have cost not more than 15-20 crores, but the Metro trains would cause the drainage off at least 8000 crores!.'

areas. As its geography expanded formally, its rickshaw-drivers increased in numbers informally. Today the rickshaw-drivers have turned into a new community and a new class. Knowingly or unknowingly, they are intervening in the changes taking place in the definition of modernity. Behind their positive intervention in the urban life of Delhi are those promises of the 'NCR project' that are yet to be fulfilled and which don't seem to be getting fulfilled in the near future.

Capital, Zone and Region

It is an undeniable fact that Delhi got the maximum attention after our freedom. As the largest industrial city of north India and also the institutionalised centre of parliamentary politics, it provided maximum opportunities for education, employment and health services. With indicators like highest per capita income in the country, low tax rates and taxation on fewer commodities Delhi appealed to the imagination of the entire country. Hence whoever needed to or whoever felt ambitious enough, moved towards Delhi. This included those upper caste

people who came in search of money and fame as well as those village people who having lost their land and ordinary means of livelihood due to changing production-relations wanted to begin their struggle for life afresh sought refuge in the city. It was one of the aims of the 'NCR project' to stave off these incoming people into the adjacent areas. Apart from this the project wanted to transfer all offices barring the main government ones into these very adjacent areas. By decentralising industries, it wanted to scatter the industries in such a manner so that any particular area didn't have to bear the brunt and the entire region could industrialise uniformly. The poor 'basties' of the metro areas of this region too were to be rehabilitated in such a manner that the slum-dwellers would not have to undergo the difficulties of displacement and their standard of life too would improve in the new place.

Pre-rickshaw driving Occupations: Abandoned under the duress

Hence, 1,483 sq. km. area of Delhi was termed as NCT. To make this territory into a region, a 13,413 sq. km. area was added to the boundary of Delhi by assimilating Panipat tehsil of Panipat district along with Haryana's Faridabad, Gurgaon, Rohtak, Sonipat and Rewari districts. To the other boundary of Delhi, an area of 4,493 sq. km. was added by assimilating the Alwar, Ramgarh, Bahror,

Kishangarh, Mandawar and Tijara tehsils of Alwar district. Similarly, to the third boundary of Delhi an area of 10,853 sq. km. belonging to Meerut, Ghaziabad and Bulandshahar districts of Uttar Pradesh was added. A plan to develop Hisar from Haryana, Gwalior from Madhya Pradesh, Patiala from Punjab, Kota from Rajasthan and Bareli from Uttar Pradesh as 'counter magnets' to the capital was conceived as well. Gurgaon, Faridabad, Noida, Ghaziabad, Bahadurgarh and Narela were considered as parts of the metro area. In this way a plan of creating a larger geography by adding different geographies of 6,677 villages and 94 cities was made but it was necessary to install a fit, fast, modern and developed transport system within and among these zones in order to make it a well organised unit. A plan was made for this area armed with road, water, train and air ways to run fast moving electric trains by turning the single line into a double one so that the working people going to Delhi from the adjacent areas found it convenient to travel. The plan to construct the metro train within Delhi is also part of this plan so that the city could be saved from pollution. The plan was to create a net of roads in such a way that people could travel from one area of the region to the other without entering Delhi

Pre-rickshaw driving Occupations: Abandoned under the duress

at all.

At first glance it appears that institutionalising Delhi as the centre and the adjacent areas as periphery is the aim of NCR. The relation between the centre and the periphery is a hierarchical one. It is necessary for the centre to retain its identity by retaining the periphery as periphery. In this manner the phenomenon of marginalisation comes to fore. It is not coincidental that the plan of this region began to take effect from 1989 onwards and from 1991, large-scale changes in the national life began to take place due to the ideological pressures of globalisation.

By the time the 20th century got over, even the minimum ideological objections to the theory of peripheralisation melted away. In order to make Delhi more beautiful, pollution-free and conforming to the international standards, orders were passed to shift the industrial units away from the city which took away the means of livelihood of lakhs of labourers. The lives of millions of people dependent on them got unsettled. Similarly, thousands of people became unemployed due to the order replacing diesel and petrol

Pre-rickshaw driving Occupations: Abandoned under the duress

Women Empowerment and the Rickshaw

Early morning some men and women are drawing towards the fields of Burari Ibrahimpur and Nathupura, some of them are on foot and some on carts. Paddling the cart, ringing the bell women too are advancing towards the Yamuna.

Where did these women derive inspiration for driving the rickshaw carts? The government aimed at turning Delhi into a cyber city. It emphasised upon the computer-literacy of women. From the buttons of computers, then, how could their fingers slip on to the handles of the rickshaw?

Oblivious of the CM's blueprint of their empowerment, these women keep terribly occupied. They are busy slashing fodder, feeding and cleaning cattle, fetching grass and vegetable from and cowdung to the fields. In addition to these drudgeries they cook, prepare cowdung chips and fetch water. All this demands time and energy. Cart-rickshaws add to their efficiency level multi-fold. And thus the pair of women and cart-rickshaws!

From the Yamuna banks these women fetch vegetables, lime, and melons etc. to sell in the local haats. One of them says, 'Waiting for the assistance of men is pointless. The times have changed! Why not drive one's own rickshaw? Rickshaw helps us run the business smoothly.' Another woman declares, 'With a rickshaw around my efficiency has increased four fold.' The third one says, 'Leaving everything on men would also reduce our income by half. Why waste time and lag behind ?'

When women can excel in offices, factories, politics and professional institutes—why not try their hand at business like these? Only 17 per cent of the wives of Delhi's rickshaw-drivers are engaged in business. This number is a little more than 23.3 per cent in Delhi and the least (12.3 per cent) in UP City-life is costlier, so women here venture out more.

7.8 per cent of such women are employed in factories, 23.1 per cent in *kothies*, 9.8 per cent are self-employed, 3.4 per cent of them are in service-sector, 2 per cent of them are daily-wagers and 48 per cent are house wives who indulge in agrarian work also. The percentage of women working as agrarian labourers is 54.6 per cent in Delhi and 77 per cent in Rajasthan.

Most of them are wedded to rickshaw-drivers. Not a single of the Rajasthani women works in a factory. 1.4 per cent of women are attached to factories in Delhi, 11.5 per cent in Haryana and 8.6 per cent in UP Compared to the wives of migrant labourers living in Delhi with their respective families, the wives of those living alone work harder. They work mostly in villages. Most of the Rajasthani rickshaw-drivers return to neighbouring villages almost every evening. That's how the percentage of working wives here is greater.

with CNG.

Looking through the eyes of a rickshaw-driver this hierarchical division of centre, periphery and marginalisation emerges in a very complex manner. For example, rickshaws were banned from plying in most parts in order to turn Delhi into one of the most modern cities of the world. Delhi is divided into three independent administrative bodies: Delhi Municipal Corporation, New Delhi Municipal Council and Delhi Cantonment Council. Along with this, the entire city has also been divided into red, yellow and green zones. While rickshaws cannot move at all in the red zone, there cannot ply between 8 in the morning and 11 in the night in the yellow zone. They can ply without any hindrance in the green zone alone. The New Delhi Municipal Council comes fully under the red zone. This is the area where all the institutions of parliamentary democracy are located and the people governing this country in the form of the parliamentarians and officers reside over here. Hence this part is the super centre of the centre of Delhi. Through the means of rules and regulations this centre has pushed the rickshaw into its peripheries.

If all the cars, scooters, motor-cycles and buses of Mumbai, Bangalore, Kolkata and Chennai are added together even then they can't equal the numbers in Delhi. Keeping the popularity of these fast driven vehicles in mind, Delhi is soon being transformed into a city which will have the maximum number of flyovers while the attempt will be to remove all the red lights on the entire ring road. The roads are being smoothened and beautified accordingly. On the other hand the condition of the lanes and streets of other urban areas of the region is quite pathetic. There is no prohibition against the rickshaw out here but driving rickshaws on battered and pot-holed roads is extremely difficult and backbreaking. There is considerable amount of chaos on these streets due to the absence of any kind of traffic control. Rickshaw-drivers have to pay for this.

The increasing number of motor-driven vehicles is continuously eating into the incomes of rickshaw-drivers. Evidently, the difficulties of the rickshaw are increasing. Yet the number of those driving it continues to rise. Whether legal or illegal, if the number of 6 lakh rickshaws plying in the urban areas of the entire region along with mechanics, owners, those involved in its production and their families are added together, the strength of this community will increase considerably. If the rickshaw has managed to maintain its space in this process despite obstacles created by the process of urbanisation then the biggest reason for this is that the poverty of the countryside pushes people towards the cities and there is always space for them in the margins that serve the centre of the city.

As a metropolis the special thing about Delhi is that about 42 per cent of its population in the 1990s consisted of non-Delhiwallahs, which had crossed the mark of 50 per cent by 1995. In this way Delhi gradually became a city of those who had come here after being uprooted from their lands in some or the other manner. Among these uprooted people, are those earning Rs. 1 lakh per month through jobs in the IT sector as well as those rickshaw-drivers earning between Rs. 2,500 to 3,500 per month. In fact the role of the rickshaw-drivers in making the universal character of Delhi cannot be overestimated. The only difference between IT and riding a rickshaw is that a computer specialist knowingly leaves his/her roots in search of money and prosperity while the rickshaw-driver is forced to leave his land due to poverty and lack of resources.

Everybody loves her/his land. One wants to go to far off places only under some compulsions. Rickshaw-drivers in NCR have left their villages mainly due to two reasons—almost 51 per cent due to unemployment and about 35 per cent because they were unable to make their ends meet in their erstwhile professions. Among the rest some left their villages due to loss in their business, some due to less wages, some due to famine or flood, some others due to unavailability of work of their choice, increase in the debt-burden and some in search of a better life.

Whether permanent or temporary rickshaw-drivers, all go to their villages. Only those who have now permanently settled in the towns of NCR and who don't have any parental property any more, don't go to their villages. There is no logic in the original inhabitants of the city going to the village. A few come to the city from their villages everyday and ply rickshaws and return to their villages. These people belong to those adjacent villages that have some or the other vehicle of transport available to them or the distance is such that it can be covered on foot. These villages either come within the ambit of NCR or are adjacent to it and 43.6 per cent of those going to the villages do some or the other work once they are back in their village. Out of these about 49 per cent do their own farming while about 36 per cent perform labour in the fields.

Approximately 9 per cent go for other kinds of labour. Some of them even engage in self-employment, animal husbandry and domestic work etc. A few of them drive the rickshaw for a few days in adjacent towns after reaching their villages. This fact is accepted by 2.3 per cent in the Haryana sub-region and 1.5 per cent in the Delhi sub-region. A few others engage in some other kinds of work.

Uprooted People, Cosmopolitanism and Poverty

If the meaning of cosmopolitanism is multi-cultural citizenship free from the primacy of religion and caste then the certificate for this kind of citizenship should first go to the rickshaw-drivers of Delhi though most of them don't possess any kind of certificate proving their citizenship. A glance at the source of the rickshaw-drivers would show that the number of people residing in original Delhi is very small. Among them about 38 per cent belong to Bihar and same percentage to Uttar Pradesh. One or two per cent people can be found from Nepal, Madhya Pradesh, Uttaranchal, Jharkhand and Orissa. A few Bangladeshis are plying the rickshaw too. Somebody left his village because of loss in the business, some due to lesser wages, some others due to lack of work of one's choice, and some in order to escape from bonded labour. The most frequent reason behind their coming to Delhi is that they already had a relative or someone their village in the city.

Rickshaw driving is a paternal profession for less than 1

per cent of the people. Most rickshaw-drivers come from rural or semi-urban poor backgrounds. It would be rare to find a category of professions traditionally associated with the poor, which doesn't contain people earning their livelihood by driving the rickshaw. fifty three per cent rickshaw-drivers of the region either have been agricultural labourers or have earned their livelihood through some other kind of labour. Out of these, 35 per cent come are poor peasants and 4 per cent are associated with some or the other traditional service. The number of rickshaw-drivers from Uttar Pradesh and Bihar in the entire region has been almost equal, 38 per cent each. But there is considerable difference in their numbers from the point of view of their original place in the different sub-regions of the region. The Bihari rickshaw-drivers in Haryana and Uttar Pradesh are 43 and 31 per cent respectively. But in the Rajasthan sub-region they are only 3.4 per cent. In Delhi they are quite a lot—49.2 per cent i.e. almost half. In the Uttar Pradesh sub-region of people from UP and in the Rajasthan sub-region people from Rajasthan are in a majority. Their percentage is 62.8 and 92 per cent respectively. Rickshaw-drivers originally belonging to UP now in Delhi are about 39 per cent. But the percentage of Haryanavi and Rajasthani rickshaw-drivers is very small here.

Rickshaw-drivers from both the states would be about 0.8 per cent each. Though Rajasthani rickshaw-drivers in the Haryana sub-region are 6.6. per cent but in UP they are found only rarely. Bengali rickshaw-drivers are maximum in the Haryana sub-region—9.1 per cent. In Delhi and UP they are about 3.8 and 2 per cent. The reason behind their absence in the Rajasthan sub-region is that Alwar or Bhiwadi have not been developed properly, hence these towns don't manage to attract labourers from outside the state very often. And the local people from these cities get more opportunities in the rickshaw sector. Barring the Rajasthan sub-region, rickshaw-drivers from Nepal, MP, Uttaranchal, Jharkhand and Orissa are between 1.5 per cent in other sub-regions. A few Bangladeshis too are plying rickshaws in NCR but don't reveal their identities clearly. Generally they call themselves Bengali or Assamese. The main reason behind this is that they are perpetually fearful of the danger of being forced by the administration to leave India. Unlike the Nepalese, the Bangladeshis can't earn their livelihood freely in India, as the laws of Bangladesh and India don't permit them to do so. While thinking about the social structure of rickshaw-drivers it is important to keep in mind that it only gives bare information about them. It is not a homogenous indicator of a specific group of rickshaw-drivers in this region, sub-region or some specific town. For example, Sikh rickshaw-drivers are more in numbers only in the city of Alwar. To find them in towns like Loni or Hodal would be an exception indeed. Similarly, a specific group of rickshaw-drivers cannot be found dispersed in the entire city. For example, Bengali rickshaw-drivers are in large numbers in one or two localities in Gurgaon but not even a single one is to be found in other localities. This kind of care has to be taken while trying to understand all other percentages.

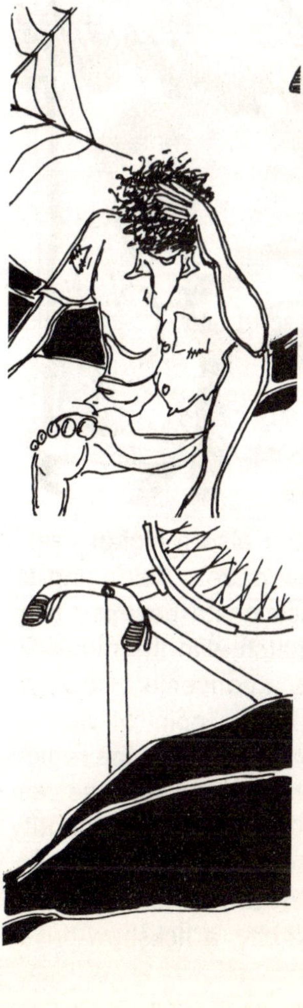

People driving rickshaws in the region come here mainly because they know somebody already residing here. They think that they will find some work after reaching here. People have come to all the sub-regions barring the Rajasthan in this manner. They are three-fourth in number. People from the Rajasthan sub-region have come to this place because this falls nearer home. Such people are about 66 per cent in number. People coming to find work on their own are most in Delhi sub-region (15.2 per cent). Very few come because of a bigger income or transfer of their guardians. But the number of rickshaw-drivers coming due to the transfer of their guardians is not small. They are almost 6 per cent.

This study of the social and communitarian inclination of rickshaw-drivers in the region makes it abundantly clear that despite having come from different castes, religions, communities, languages, dialects and cultures, they are all being forced to take on the garb of cosmopolitanism within the margins of the city. This is evidence in itself of the way in which the conditions are taking them towards modernisation unwittingly. The lower castes, especially the untouchables look towards the city as a place where no one will ask them their caste and they will be able to don the identity of a citizen. It is clear that no customer asks a rickshaw-driver his caste, but fellow rickshaw-drivers do. The specific Indian attitude of looking down upon the profession of rickshaw driving stops not only a lower caste rickshaw-driver but also a higher caste one from divulging his caste. Rickshaw-drivers belonging to higher castes shy away from telling their caste because they find this labouring profession doesn't match with the ritualistic standards of their caste. The city draws a convenient cover of anonymity over their caste identity. From the point of view of religion, about three-fourth of the rickshaw-drivers of the region are Hindus, a little less than one-fourth Muslims and the rest consist of other religious groups but their religious identity doesn't mean anything to them.

The religion of the rickshaw-driver is his rickshaw. Carrying customers on the roads of the city, a rickshaw-driver creates such a world by combining his sweat and the wage in lieu of it, where caste and religion become irrelevant. In this respect he is different from the middleclass Delhiwallah because a middleclass Delhite never detaches himself from his caste and religious identity. He even creates his ghetto in the cosmopolitanism of the metropolis and tries to participate in all kinds of communitarian conflicts. It is not that a rickshaw-wallah does not possess caste or religious consciousness. He

Aspects of a Rickshaw-driver's life

may have been seen to be taking interest in the 'jagratas' in the city, especially Delhi. But eventually his profession and life-conditions obliterate such forms of consciousness. Also, most of the rickshaw-drivers are young who are more pliable to change. The structure of tradition is not so deeply embedded in their minds that their lines could not be washed out.

The Family of a Rickshaw-driver

One should not conclude that rickshaw-drivers don't main-

Aspects of a rickshaw-driver's life

tain material links with their native place. But, a glance through their family lives reveals that the communitarian tendencies are less influential in their link with their original places, which is more closely tied to personal relations. Three-fourth of the rick-shaw-drivers are married. More than half of these (56.5 per cent) stay alone in the city. The reason for their staying alone is that they want to save maximum money and send it to their dependants at home. They think that a large share of their

Aspects of a Rickshaw-driver's life

income will be spent on house rent and other necessities if they stay with their families, whereas they already have a house for the family back in their village. Rickshaw-drivers living alone doesn't mean that they live a lonely life. In fact they live with their friends as a group in the city and never feel loneliness. Also the cost of living and eating per person becomes minimum. Since Delhi is more expensive compared to the other areas of the region, rickshaw-drivers here make maxi-

Aspects of a rickshaw-driver's life

mum sacrifices. They have to face maximum hardships. but even then 73.7 per cent rickshaw-drivers live alone in the metropolis. As far as the family is concerned if Delhi has the maximum number of rickshaw-drivers living alone then the married ones are the most in the Rajasthan sub-region i.e. 81.6 per cent. One doesn't need to say that most of the rickshaw-drivers in this area are locals instead of displaced. The tendency to live with the family too is maximum here (87.4 per cent). Most of the rickshaw-drivers either belong to this town or are from nearby villages. Despite residing at some distance, they come everyday to the city to drive rickshaw and go back to their homes after work.

One-fourth of the rickshaw-drivers in the entire region are either unmarried (21 per cent) or widowers (2.5 per cent). Almost 7 per cent among the minor rickshaw-drivers too are married. Those living with their families in the city are about 43.5 per cent. About 70.5 of those living alone i.e. 56.5 per cent, are married. The tendency of living away from the family is more in those above 30 years of age. The number of rick-

shaw-drivers in this age group too is high (67.6 per cent). But with the increase in the age the tendency to live with the family grows too. Only 46.6 per cent among the age group 31-40 years and 37.3 per cent in the age group above this live alone. This means that rickshaw-drivers from the younger age group think more about saving money.

Only 46.4 per cent of the rickshaw-drivers in the region send money to their homes, 74 per cent of Delhi and 5.7 in the Rajasthan sub-region send money to their homes. Mostly those living alone do this. But it will be a mistake to think that everybody living alone would be sending money to his home. Actually of those living alone, 74.3 per cent send money home but 25.7 per cent don't. The probable reason behind this is that they don't earn enough to be able to save money after meeting their personal needs. On the other hand, there are about 10.3 per cent who despite living with their families send money to their native places. This manifests the drive of the joint family in Indian society.

Out of those rickshaw-drivers who live with their families some of them are unmarried (12.3 per cent) and some are widowed (2.2 per cent). It is only to suggest that the rickshaw-drivers consist both of individual and joint families. The money sent by rickshaw-drivers to their home is not a big amount. Out of all those who send money from the region, almost 70 per cent send between Rs. 1000 and 1500. The percentage of rickshaw-drivers sending money from Delhi is comparatively less i.e. 65.5 per cent. But there are about 13 per cent rickshaw-drivers out here who send money between Rs. 1500 and 2000. About 3 per cent send between Rs. 2000 and 3000 and about 1 per cent send more than this amount. The upper limit for the money sent by rickshaw-drivers from Rajasthan, Uttar Pradesh and Haryana is Rs. 1500, 2000 and 3000 respectively.

Earnings, Savings and Expenditure

The everyday earning of rickshaw-drivers is not fixed. But about 86 per cent earn between Rs. 50 and 100. The percentage of these rickshaw-drivers in Haryana and the Delhi sub-region is 93.7 and 65.9 per cent. From the point of view of the region the first is the maximum and the second the minimum percentage. There are around 1 per cent or fewer rickshaw-drivers who earn less than Rs. 50 and 13.3 per cent (in Delhi 33.8 per cent) who earn more than Rs. 100. Subtracting the everyday rent of the rickshaw, cost of transport from the residence to the work place and vice versa, tea and biri etc. out of this amount they are left with very little money. After subtracting the cost of food and other necessities about 3.6 per cent rickshaw-drivers in the region (about 33.3 per cent in the Rajasthan subregion) are left with nothing, 40.7 per cent save less than Rs. 50, 55 per cent between 50 and 100 and 0.7 per cent rickshaw-drivers save more than Rs. 100.

Most of them (about 86 per cent) keep their savings with them; some with their friends and acquaintances and some with the rickshaw-owners. One per cent go to banks. Of course, the monthly savings of a rickshaw-driver is nothing but a sum of his everyday savings. 28.4 per cent rickshaw-drivers don't manage to save anything, 18 per cent less than Rs. 1000 and 39.5 per cent (in Delhi 49.3 per cent) from Rs. 1000 to Rs. 1500. And 14 per cent rickshaw-drivers save over Rs. 1500. They use this money in different ways 41.4 per cent of those living with their families spend it in their homes. 52.7 per cent of those living away from their homes send it there. Some of them (3.5 per cent) keep it with themselves and some others (2 per cent) spend it on themselves.

Despite this, some of them have to borrow money once in a while. There are about 30.6 per cent such rickshaw-drivers. Most of them take money as debt from their relatives and friends. Some of them borrow even from moneylender. Those borrowing in these two manners are 67.5 per cent and 29.8 per cent respectively and 12.6 per cent rickshaw-drivers confessed to have borrowed less than Rs. 500, 37.8 per cent between Rs. 500-1000, 16.9 per cent between Rs. 1-2000, 10.7 per cent between Rs. 2-4000, 15.95 per cent between Rupees 4 to 10000, and 6 per cent over Rs. 10,000. There were many reasons for borrowing money. Those who borrowed for marriage, illness, house-construction, buying rickshaw, sending home, individual or family spending and other heads are respectively: 5.9, 50.7, 4.2, 8.2, 12.8, 14.5 and 3.9. forty seven per cent of the rickshaw-drivers don't have to pay any interest on this debt. But about 38.5 per cent have to pay with the rate between 2 to 5 per cent, 12.9 per cent have to pay ranging 5 and 10 per cent and about 1 per cent rickshaw-drivers have to pay interest with the rate of over 10 per cent. The biggest problem a rickshaw-driver faces after coming to the city is finding a home. Where do the rickshaw-drivers of the region stay—it depends on their economic conditions, room rent in the place of the work, the distance between the work place and their village or the place of origin and the location of their acquaintances residing in that city etc.

The Residence of the Rickshaw-driver

Some of the rickshaw-drivers live in their rooms, some in their slums, some in rickshaw-garages or some on the foot-path. For this, they don't have to pay rent. Some of the people stay in rented rooms or in the slums. Some of them stay in a temple, with some acquaintance or even in a school. About 76 per cent rickshaw-drivers in the Rajasthan sub-region live in their own rooms or homes. But only 15 per cent from the Haryana sub-region, 24 per cent from the UP sub-region and only 5 per cent in the Delhi sub-region live in their own homes. While 10.4 per cent rickshaw-drivers from the UP sub-region live in garages the percentage of such rickshaw-drivers in the Delhi sub-region is 8.8 per cent.

Rickshaw-drivers in Haryana, UP, and Delhi sub-regions have their own slums. Their percentage respectively is 4.2, 3.8 and 2.5. Similarly the percentage of those living in rented slums in these sub-regions is 2.2, 2.3 and 3 per cent respectively. But in the Rajasthan sub-region no one has either his own slum or rented one. The percentage of those living in the rented rooms is 65 per cent in Haryana, 48.8 per cent in UP, 17.2 per cent in Rajasthan and 64.4 per cent in the Delhi sub-regions. The percentage of those sleeping on the footpath or on their rickshaws in these sub-regions is 9.4 per cent, 5.4 per cent, 3.4 per cent and 14.1 per cent respectively.

The lack of public toilets or their unsuitability even in the case of availability is a big problem. As a result they defecate in the open. There is complete lack of public toilets in the Rajasthan sub-region. Only 7 per cent rickshaw-drivers have their own toilets, while the remaining 93 per cent defecate in the open. The percentage of such people in the Haryana sub-region is 68.4 and in UP sub-region it is 56.3 per cent. Though this percentage is relatively low (38.6) in Delhi, yet it amounts to more than 1.5 lakh rickshaw-drivers. The percentage of those using their own toilets in the Haryana, UP and Delhi sub-regions is 31, 40.3 and 45.7 respectively, 15.7 per cent rickshaw-drivers use public toilets in Delhi but in Haryana and U.P. sub-regions only 0.6 and 3.3 per cent use them. There is usually a long queue in public toilets and they have to pay money for the service. Because of this they try to avoid public toilets. Even those renting out slums or the rooms don't arrange for such facilities. Hence they have to use open fields, 50.5 per cent of those living in rented rooms use open fields, 47.1 per cent use their own toilets and 2.5 per cent use public toilets. Out of those living in rented slums 80.8 per cent use open fields, 7.7 per cent use their own toilets and 11.5 per cent use public toilets.

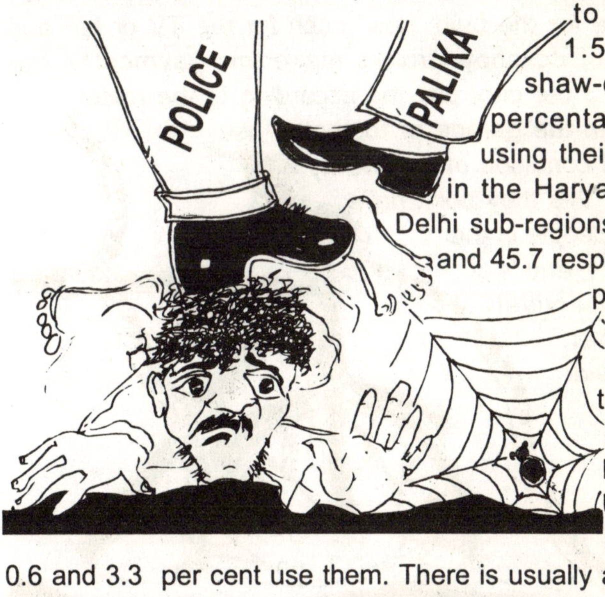

Electricity is considered to be the backbone of modern life. But just as the consumption of other utilities is the privilege of the well-off so is the case of electricity. In the Haryana, UP, Rajasthan and Delhi sub-regions about 20.7 per cent, 22.1 per cent, 14.9 per cent and 7.8 per cent don't use electricity at all because they don't have it in the first place.

Those living in rented rooms or in rented slums have to pay electricity bills along with the rent to the owners. How much a rickshaws-driver has to pay for electricity depends upon the electrical appliances (e.g. fan, TV, bulb, radio and iron etc.) used by him. The owner doesn't charge the money according to the bill but decides of his own will as to how much he will charge for the bulb, how much for the TV or fan and 52.7 per cent rickshaw-drivers make this payment in the region with 7.3 per cent pay the according to the meter. Those living in the garage or footpaths use power on the condition of availability of power. For this they don't have to pay. Such people in the region are 8.1 and 4.3 per cent respectively and 7.3 per cent steal power by using a loop in the electric wires. Some of them have to pay the electricity department or its officials for this purpose, some of them escape even paying this much as the moment the electricity department officials come on a visit, they remove their loops.

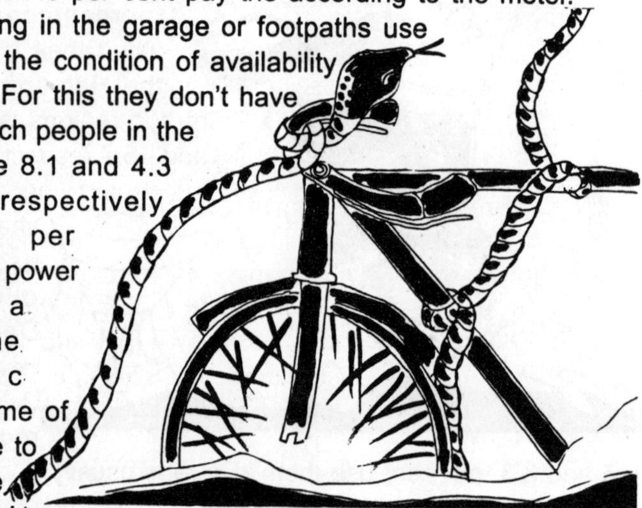

7.7 per cent use gas stoves, 43.9 per cent kerosene oil stoves and 33.5 per cent use traditional stoves to cook food. They use wood, cow dung etc. for fuel in traditional stoves. The percentage of those using gas stove is maximum in the UP sub-region (10.9 per cent). Those using kerosene oil are maximum in Delhi (66.9 per cent). The users of traditional fuel are

maximum in Rajasthan (88.5 per cent). Those rickshaw-drivers who use gas stoves usually live with their families and have higher incomes. Those using kerosene oil in Delhi have to procure it from the black market, where they have to pay a higher amount. They don't have ration cards; hence they don't get oil from the ration depots. Those eating at their friends' or relatives' places don't have to manage their own fuel. The percentage of such rickshaw-drivers is average and 14.7 per cent rickshaw-drivers eat food in cheap hotels or dhabas in the entire region. They too don't have to collect fuel.

Rickshaw Driving is Another Name of Helplessness

All those coming from the far off countryside don't begin to drive rickshaws immediately after reaching Delhi. Only about half of those driving rickshaws in the region are the ones who coincidentally, out of choice or under some compulsion began with rickshaw-driving. The percentage of such people is only slightly higher in the Haryana sub-region (52 per cent) and slightly less in the Delhi sub-region (43 per cent).

Twenty one per cent rickshaw-driver in the region began their urban life as a daily wage labourers, while 12.5 per cent as factory labourers, 16.1 per cent in the Rajasthan sub-region and 14.6 per cent in the Delhi sub-region began working as factory labourers, while 24.1 per cent in the UP sub-region and 17.7 per cent in the Delhi sub-region began working as daily wage labourers. Some of them began through self-employment while some others through a job. Delhi has the highest percentage of both these in the entire region, 8.6 and 13.4 per cent respectively. They also looked for their future in motor-driving and even other kinds of works. While 2.3 per cent are those who started as rickshaw-drivers in the Rajasthan sub-region, 1.8 per cent began through other work in the Delhi sub-region. They are the highest percentages in these two areas in the entire region. It is true that due to less wages in different kinds of work, closure of factories, irregularity of jobs, ill-behaviour of employers, loss in business, expulsion from jobs, transfer of factories people begin to ply rickshaws. But this is equally true that people also begin to ply rickshaws due to individual freedom, paternal profession and somebody known already in the same profession.

A Legally Run Illegal Profession

Rickshaw driving is a profession, which is run illegally despite it being a legal profession. There is a need for a license for the rickshaw-driver and the rickshaw in some towns of NCR while in others it is not necessary. In those towns where a license is needed, not all the rickshaw-drivers get it. According to the survey, only 20.7 per cent of them are license holders in this region. A large section of the drivers, thus, are without licenses. They all have different reasons for this. Some of them (10.9 per cent) don't even know where the license is made, 44.5 per cent tell that you don't get a license made here and 22.6 per cent say that here you don't need license. 7.9 per cent attributed this to non-issuance of the license during the survey-period and 5.2 per cent accused the civic body for not issuing the license. 1.4 per cent cited lack of money as the reason while about 5 per cent attributed this to their irregular rickshaw-driving. This was all about a license for rickshaw-drivers. But this is true as well that alongwith the license for a rickshaw-driver, a license is also, issued for the rickshaw itself. Those who have their rickshaws get it made themselves. Those who rent the rickshaw get it made by the owners. The rickshaw-owner gets the license made under the name of one or the other rickshaw-driver but it remains under the rickshaw-owner. Later only that person under whose name it is registered does not drive that rickshaw. Legally rickshaw-owners cannot keep more than one rickshaw. But it becomes possible with the connivance of officials of the Municipal Corporation and rickshaw-owners that many rickshaw-owners own many (even hundreds) rickshaws. 52.5 per cent rickshaw-drivers said that the rickshaws they were driving were authorised. About 19 per cent accepted that they weren't, 26.7 per cent said that the authorisation process had stopped while 2 per cent gave other reasons including that authorisation was not done there. Neither the unlicensed rickshaws are allowed on the streets nor the unlicensed rickshaw-drivers are allowed to ride licensed or unlicensed rickshaws. Officials of civic bodies keep launching movements to impound unlicensed rickshaws very frequently. Practically only those rickshaws are caught whose owners haven't paid a bribe though the reason given is no license for the rickshaw or the driver. But not all the rickshaws meet this fate - 20.4 per cent rickshaws in the entire region have accepted having got their rickshaws caught at least once. 14.3 per cent of these took recourse to bribery. According to 56.5 per cent (88.6 per cent in Delhi) the owners got them released. About 26 per cent said that in order to get the rickshaw released immediately license had to be made, 3.3 per cent got it released through some connection or in some other manner. There are other reasons apart from license for the impounding of rickshaws. License is not necessary in the entire Rajasthan region. Hence the civic bodies don't impound them any more. But in the other three regions this practice continues. Ninety per cent (96.2 per cent in the UP sub-region) out of those whose rickshaws were caught cited the lack of license behind their seizure, 7.7 per cent (19.3 per cent in Delhi) cited the oldness of the rickshaw as the reason for its impounding and 1.8 per cent (2.6 per cent in Delhi) felt that their rickshaws were caught without any reason. 1.3 per cent rickshaw-drivers in UP cited other reasons behind the seizure of their rickshaws.

The Health of the Rickshaw-driver

Driving a cycle-rickshaw demands hard labour. People generally put a lot of heavy luggage on the rickshaw. About three-four people sit on the rickshaw along with their luggage. People who generally take a ride on the rickshaw belong to the middle class or such background whose economic condition is not very good. They normally behave like this in order to save money. The rickshaw-driver doesn't say no in the hope of good money. The result is that he has to use more force in order to drive the rickshaw and suffers on health grounds.

Rickshaw-drivers from Haryana, Uttar Pradesh, Rajasthan and Delhi 12.8, 7, 12.6 and 32.8 respectively said they had fallen sick. Three-fourth of these went to the doctor and about 21 per cent took some help from a chemist and took some medicine. Some of them went to their villages and got treatment there. Rickshaw-drivers of all the sub-regions, Haryana, Uttar Pradesh, Rajasthan and Delhi, rarely use government hospitals. They normally go to the private doctors. The percentage of those treated by the private doctors in these sub-regions is 82.7, 84.8, 46 and 91.7 per cent respectively. Those taking medicines from government hospitals and medical stores are 6.9 and 6.6 per cent respectively - almost equal. These people manage to get themselves treated with their own savings or on borrowed - money. 96.8 per cent use their savings and 2.8 per cent borrow money to get treatment. 19.4, 19.6, 37.0 and 8.6 per cent from the Haryana, UP, Rajasthan and Delhi sub-regions accepted that their rickshaw-owners helped them during illness. This help comes in many forms—monetary, not taking rent on the off day and not harassing later for rent etc.

The body comes under strain from driving the rickshaw.

Different parts of the body suffer pain because of it. Rickshaws suffer from fever, breathlessness, weakness and other kinds of diseases. Rickshaw-drivers tell many such tales and 58.2 per cent talk openly about the ill-effects of driving the rickshaw. Out of these, 78.4 per cent complain of body pain, 16.5 per cent of weakness, 3.2 per cent of breath-related ailments, 1.1 per cent of fever and the rest become victims of other diseases. In any case, weakness always accompanies them. Most of the rickshaw-drivers (41.3 per cent) feel tired after having driven the rickshaw for one to two hours, while 14.8 per cent feel the same after two to three hours, 20.6 per cent after three to four hours, 19.8 per cent after five-six hours while 3.5 per cent don't feel tired at all.

Why doesn't the rickshaw-wallah buy his own rickshaw?

According to the rule books of civic bodies most of the rickshaw-drivers should have their own rickshaws. But the real picture is the opposite - 37.3, 31.1, 47.1 and 14.4 per cent rickshaw-drivers in the Haryana, U.P., Rajasthan and Delhi sub-regions respectively have their own rickshaws, while 62.7, 68.9, 52.9 and 85.6 per cent drive the rented rickshaws respectively. There are many reasons for this. Rickshaw-drivers can hardly manage to take care of their basic needs like foods and clothes saving is not possible for all rickshaw-drivers. Even if they have money, they need some place to park their rickshaw. Poor people can barely manage a place for themselves. Most of the rickshaw-drivers live in one room which they share with many. Getting the rickshaw passed from the civic body is also quite tough. Officials demand money for the same. Without bribe no license is issued for the rickshaw or its driver. Many come here with the thought that they are going to be here for a very short time, hence are unwilling to purchase the rickshaw thinking what will they do with it when they return to the village. Many such things dissuade a rickshaw-driver from becoming an owner himself. Those in a better financial situation or with a strong desire to purchase a rickshaw do so. Those keeping their own rickshaws in the region (70.7 per cent) do so with their own money, 20.5 per cent buy it through a financier or the producer on regular instalments. Some of them borrow money from their friends, relatives or some acquaintances to buy a rickshaw,. 3.5 per cent rickshaw-drivers in Delhi have borrowed money from the bank for this purpose. But this category is not found in the other sub-regions.

Those plying a rickshaw on rent have to furnish a bond to the owner. Barring a few exceptions most of the rickshaw-drivers do this. This bond is not in the written form. When a rickshaw-driver goes to the owner to take the rickshaw for the first time he takes another person with him who knows both of them. On the recommendation of this person alone does the driver get his rickshaw. Generally this third person is somebody who has already taken a rickshaw on rent from the owner at some point of time.

The rickshaw-driver takes the rickshaw from the owner on a daily rent. This rent ranges between Rs. 10 to Rs. 30. The rent is fixed on the basis of mainly two things—whether the rickshaw is old or new i.e. what is the condition of the rickshaw. An older rickshaw fetches less rent compared to the new one. And second, what is the scale of living in the concerned city. Very often the rent is higher in the bigger cities as against the small towns. Those paying rent between Rs. 12-15 in the Haryana, UP, Rajasthan and Delhi sub-regions respectively are 48.4, 66.6, 39.1 and 11.5 per cent while those paying between Rs, 15-20 are 46.3, 26.6, 41.3 and 72.6 per cent respectively, while 15.3 per cent rickshaw-drivers in Delhi pay a rent between Rs. 20-25. Those paying between Rs. 25-30 during the survey were 0.6 per cent. The number of rickshaws with new body (iron body) is increasing fast these days. Their rent is the same. Normally the responsibility for the upkeep of the rented rickshaw is with the owner, though some rickshaw-drivers take this upon themselves. Hence 96 per cent owners in Delhi do the same while 19.6 per cent rickshaw-drivers in Rajasthan take this responsibility. But since there are very few rickshaws in this sub-region the number of such rickshaws is very small. According to 17.7 per cent rickshaw-drivers in the Haryana sub-region, both the owner and the driver share this burden that is highest here as compared to the other sub-regions.

Only 10.3 per cent families have more than one member who drives rickshaws. The percentage of those doing some other work along with driving a rickshaw is merely 2.1 per cent. Half of these are self-employed and the other half is in labour, job, animal husbandry and farming. They divide their time between driving a rickshaw or some other work according to their situation. While working in a job they spend the evenings or the nights with the rickshaw. This helps in augmenting their income a little bit. Most of the rickshaw-drivers in the region (93.6 per cent) drive it in the day-time while 2.1 per cent in the

night and a few (4.3 per cent) do so, whenever they find time. Two-thirds of the rickshaw-drivers do it for entire week, a little less than one-third for six days in a week and about 1.5 per cent ride the rickshaw between three to five days.

The Rickshaw-owner: An Illegal Category

The rickshaw is perhaps the only transport of modern urban life where there is no hierarchical difference between the owner and the driver in the eyes of the law. Barring a few exceptions, legally, every rickshaw-owner has to present himself as the rickshaw-driver too. It has been mentioned earlier how rickshaw driving is forced to exist illegally despite being a legalised profession. The speciality of rickshaw-owners is that despite this dangerous aspect of the business they risk their money on it. It's a business that needs small capital in which 100 rickshaws can be bought for only about Rs. 1.5 to 2 lakh. They are left wondering when despite giving employment to 100 people for such a small capital and despite fulfilling many needs of transport for urban citizens along with preserving the environment in the process, they find themselves on the wrong side of the law.

Legally a rickshaw-owner cannot keep more than one rickshaw. One can keep five rickshaws only when one is a widow or is handicapped

Evidently, most of the rickshaws owned by a rickshaw-owner are either against fictitious names or are without licenses. According to our study, the picture of the rickshaw-owner that emerges is something like this: *Owning capital between Rs. 1.5 to 2 lakh on an average, borrowing money from the financiers when short of money and getting the rickshaw assembled in Meerut, sometimes turning into a rickshaw-owner while driving the rickshaw, mostly hailing from Uttar Pradesh originally, generally of high caste, sometimes also a mechanic, better educated compared to average rickshaw-drivers, buy a mobile phone and a car after an improvement in his economic situation.*

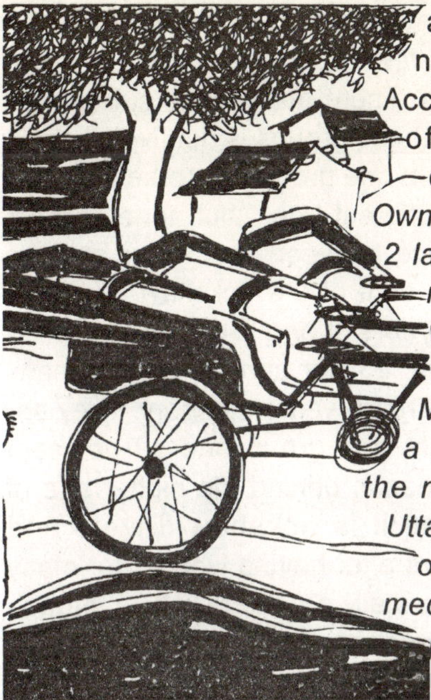

There is a lot of variation among rickshaw-owners in terms of age, caste, religion, state and background. They are the most well-off and influential part of the business. There is only one commonality among the rickshaw-owners: their business being termed illegal by the administration otherwise there is a lot of difference from person to person. There is a great amount of difference ranging from economic status to thinking. There is also a difference in the process of their becoming rickshaw owners. Geographical

conditions and changing traffic laws and restrictions by civic bodies relating to rickshaws play a major role in fixing this difference. Yet there are quite a few similarities between them. That's why they form one class. There are various sub-groups within this class. The nature of these groups is not fixed; rather, each owner keeps transiting from one group to another.

Rickshaw-owners are of different ages, but none of them is a minor. This is the difference between the owner and the driver in terms of age, 3.2 per cent of the rickshaw-drivers in the entire region are below 18 years of age. But one can rarely find a minor among the owners, 23 per cent of the rickshaw-owners in the region are in the 18-30 years category. They are 38 per cent in the 31-40 years age group and 39 per cent above 41 years. What is the reason behind the higher age of the owners? This is because it is rickshaw-drivers and mechanics, who become owners after having worked for many years. Those who are young normally get the rickshaw through inheritance, i.e., somebody has been a rickshaw-owner in their families.

From the religious point of view, 58 per cent are Hindus, 32 per cent Muslims and 8.8 per cent Sikhs. The percentage of Sikh rickshaw-owners in Haryana, UP, Rajasthan and Delhi sub-regions is 9.9, 5.3, 45.5 and 5.7 per cent respectively. In UP 1.5 per cent rickshaw-owners are Christians. This percentage is 0.6 per cent in the entire region. 9.1 per cent rickshaw-owners declined to reveal their religion in the Rajasthan sub-region. Whether Hindus or Muslims, it is mostly the higher castes who become the rickshaw-owners. Few backward caste people or Dalits among the Muslims manage to become rickshaw-owners. Despite being less in number, Sikhs generally have more rickshaws.

Compared to the drivers, the rickshaw-owners are not as illiterate. 48.6 per cent rickshaw-drivers are illiterate while only 24 per cent owners are illiterates. 8.6 per cent rickshaw-drivers are literate while they are almost double among the owners—16 per cent. Those owners educated up to primary, middle and high school level are 7.8, 14.6 and 26.9 per cent respectively

with 4.5 per cent rickshaw-owners having passed the intermediate level; 6.2 per cent of them are graduates and above. It is clear from the data that rickshaw-owners are better educated than the drivers. Because of this education, this category is more aware of its interests. If the owners are able to sustain their business despite adverse conditions then it is because of their education. Rickshaw-owners immediately take initiatives whenever government policies are publicised through the newspapers. They immediately forward their written demands to the officials in the administration. Truly speaking, this very education has helped them in becoming rickshaw-owners.

Family life holds great importance for any person. A person manages to get out of many kinds of inconveniences, frustrations and problems with the presence of his family 91.6 per cent owners are married in the region, 7.5 per cent are unmarried and 1 per cent are widowers. Almost 90 per cent owners live with their families and only 10 per cent of them live alone. The percentage of those sending money to their original homes is the same as that of those living alone. Perhaps those living with their families don't need to send money to their villages any more. Out of those who send money

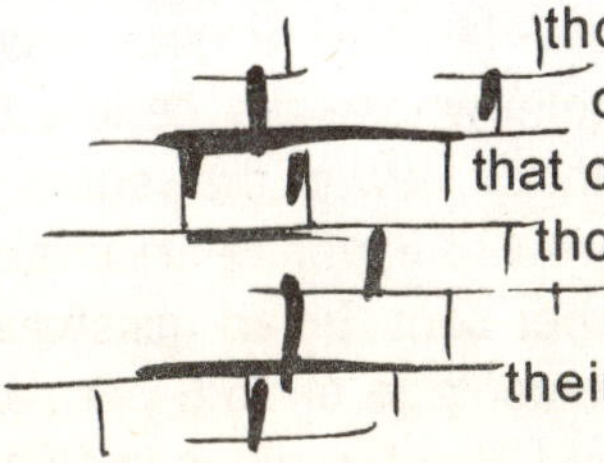

to their homes every month, about 25.9 per cent send Rs. 1000, 44.4 per cent between Rs. 1000-1500 and 29.6 per cent between Rs. 1500-2000 Wives of 96.5 per cent rickshaw-owners do not work outside their homes. Wives of rickshaw-owners in only the Haryana and UP sub-regions go out of their homes to work. Their percentage in these areas is 7.3 and 0.9 per cent respectively. This percentage is 3.5 in the entire region.

Rickshaw-owners give proper attention to the education of their children. The children of 72 per cent rickshaw-owners go to school and of 23.5 per cent don't. while 4.6 per cent owners don't have any children. Such a high percentage of school going children of rickshaw-owners has been possible due to their high educational and economic level. Rickshaw-drivers have lagged behind in terms of education and wealth. Therefore the education of their children too is not being taken care of properly. Many of them either do not understand the importance of education or even if they understand it they are not able to send their children to school due to lack of money. The economic and educational status of those rickshaw-owners whose children cannot go to school is closer to that of those rickshaw-drivers whose children don't go to school.

Most of the rickshaw-owners in NCR are originally inhabitants of Uttar Pradesh. Their percentage in the UP sub-region is 87 per cent. They are present in the Delhi and Haryana sub-regions as well. Here, they are 34.3 and 14.5 per cent respectively. The Rajasthan sub-region has rickshaw-owners only from Rajasthan and not from any other state. But Rajasthani rickshaw-owners are also in the Haryana and Delhi sub-regions. Their percentage is 2.3 and 2.9 per cent respetively.

Rickshaw-owners in Rajasthan and Haryana are not found in the Uttar Pradesh sub-region. Haryanvi rickshaw-owners are found only in Haryana and Delhi whose per cent is 60.3 and 8.6 respectively. From the point of view of the region, the percent are of Haryanavi owners (26.6 per cent) is second to those in Uttar Pradesh—47.1 per cent. Bihari rickshaw-owners are third in numbers with a percentage of 15.6 per cent. Their percent are in the Haryana and UP sub-regions is 19.1 and 9.9

respectively. Rickshaw-owners belonging to Madhya Pradesh are in UP and Delhi sub-regions and rickshaw-owners from Bengal are in the Haryana and UP sub-regions. Their percentage is about 2 per cent.

Housing is a major problem in the cities. Only one-third of the rickshaw-owners have to face this problem. Whether a room, or flat or a 'jhuggi'—most of the owners have their own place to stay. About 17 per cent live in their rooms, 45 per cent in their flats and 6.2 per cent owners live in their own 'jhuggis'. Out of these 28.6 per cent live in rented rooms, 2.6 per cent in the garage and 1 per cent in some other place. Having their own room or flat indicates their better standards of living. Half of these owners have been in this business for more than ten years. About 30 per cent have been running their rickshaws for between 1 to 5 years and 16.2 per cent between 5-10 years. Only 4.2 per cent who; have not completed even a year in this business. There are different reasons for getting into this business. Some of them chose this because they were illiterate. Such people are only in the Haryana sub-region—about 3.8 per cent and in no other area, 6.8 per cent took up this work in the region because they couldn't find any other work, 13.3 per cent are in this profession because of its being their family business 37.7 per cent chose for employment. About 10 per cent chose this job thinking it was nice work with small capital, 11.7 per cent began this work because they already had a bicycle shop or they were cycle mechanics. Some of them began this work because of lack of education,

Heavy Load on Kid Shoulders

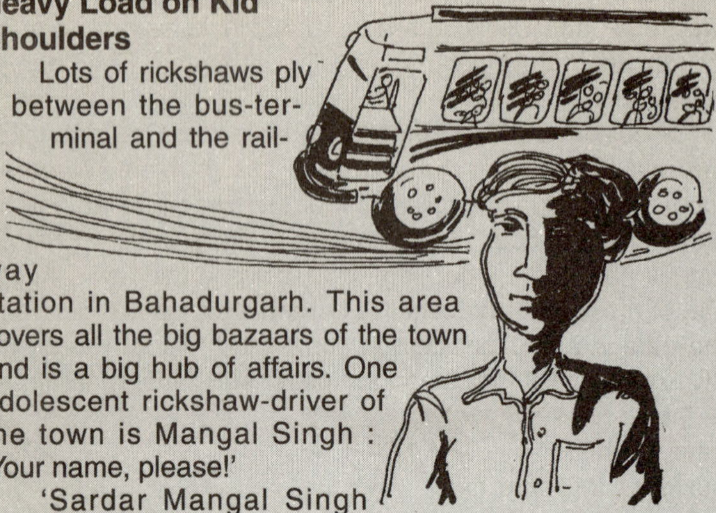

Lots of rickshaws ply between the bus-terminal and the railway station in Bahadurgarh. This area covers all the big bazaars of the town and is a big hub of affairs. One adolescent rickshaw-driver of the town is Mangal Singh : 'Your name, please!'

'Sardar Mangal Singh Arora' (with a touch of pride).

'And your age ?'

'Fifteen years.'

'Why do you pull rickshaw ?'

'My wish! For five years I was a conductor in a Teekari Border-Purani Delhi bus (route no. 926).'

'What made you switch over to this ?'

'My mood, my wish, what else ?'

'Who all are there in your family ?'

'My mother and an elder sister. We have our own house adjacent of Teekari border in Bahadurgarh. We also have a small shop of general merchandise. My sister is in class 12, my father has passed away.'

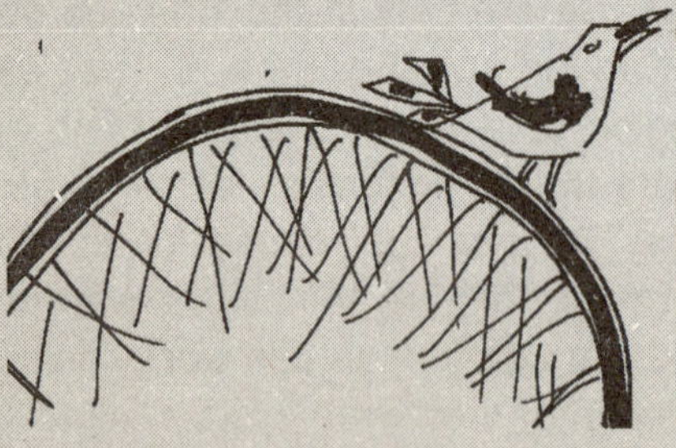

'Do you go home everyday?'

'Off and on I go there to give them money. But I sleep on the rickshaw. They think I am still a conductor.'

'Where are you from?'

'Rohtak, but for the past many years we have been in Bahadurgarh!'

Mangal has hired the rickshaw. He can be called literate, he knows his letters at least. His tone reveals that he is not happy with his family and enjoys his roving ways.

Another adolescent is Sant ram, 16. He says that he is also from Bahadurgarh, 'Everybody is earning hard in a poor family. I also contribute Rs. 50 to 60.' Sitaram Prasad of Chapra is of the same age. His mother has sent him here, he says, 'Factories do not have a place even for the elders, who would care for a kid ?'

5 per cent of the rickshaw-drivers belong to the same age group. In the age when they should be going to school, they are here on the roads!

Rickshaw on the Ceiling: Dignity of Labour

Very close to Faridabad Nagar Nigam is a party-hall called Central Green. At the entrance is the barrel of the mortar propped against a rod joining two wheels. Against the front wall a part of the jeep engine hangs. the Courtyard is green and its walls stand painted in live rural colours. Against the ceiling of this hall is suspended a huge model of the hand-pulled rickshaw. This reminds one of the Calcutta model. The puller is cast in stone. On the lower rod of the rickshaw hangs a lantern. This is not lit, still the passers have a full view of the model.

Manoj Gaba, the owner of the Central Green narrates, 'Heera Lal, one of his chowkidars was very industrious and self-respecting. During the day-time he worked as a rickshaw-puller. We knew that his presence will be short-lived but we wanted to preserve him in our memory. He was a man of his own ways. My uncle said that Heera Lal with his rickshaw looked grand. We could use him as a model but in his hands we could raise the ancient model of the man-pulled rickshaw.'

'My uncle keeps going to Kolkata He exercised his imagination and looked for a sculptor who would turn the photograph of Heera Lal holding two parallel bamboo-rods in his two hands behind him. The model of the rickshaw

was worked upon by Bhatia rickshaw-puller in NIT, no. 2.

'Initially this was placed in the Central Hall. There it drew everybody's attention. Children felt so fascinated that they came and sat straight on the rickshaw or on the shoulders of the model. In the first move this was barricaded and then hung beyond the reach of children to save it from damage and decay. For the last two years it is there on the ceiling—up above the world so high.'

Damn the Caste

In terms of caste rickshaw-drivers have lot of heterogeneity. But, 11.4 per cent of these hide their caste origin. Those belonging to the higher caste and OBCs tend to hide their caste-identity because they think driving a rickshaw is beneath their dignity and the dalits hide it for the fear of humiliation and exploitation. In fact a proper sense of democracy has yet to be inculcated among them. Only 0.8 per cent of the rickshaw-drivers say that they do not have faith in the caste system.

But, in Delhi we couldn't find a single rickshaw-driver

of this sort. 41 per cent of the rickshaw-drivers here belong to the OBC. The percentage of higher caste and the dalits is 25 per cent and 21 per cent respectively. The people belonging to the scheduled castes are negligible (0.5 per cent). Why do the people belonging to the scheduled caste prefer settling down in the neighbouring towns instead of going for far away areas? This issue has to be looked into. The percentage of OBCs and higher caste in Haryana is 46.8 per cent and 27 per cent respectively. In UP the percentage of SC is 23.4 per cent. 27 per cent of the people refusing to disclose their caste-identity in Rajasthan. This is more than in any other region. Among upper castes, 35.6 per cent people are from the Muslim upper caste. Rickshaw-driving has been proved a profession in which at least the fear of exploitation doesn't weigh heavy on the shoulders of Dalits. Unlike their native villages where they have to go through feudal oppression, here one is entirely on one's own: drive if feel like driving, otherwise stretch on the rickshaw!

My Rickshaw, My Passenger

Bamba in Meerut, PAC camp on one side of the Hapur Road. On the other side is the slum of Assamese Muslims who work as rag-pickers. Some 30 of these people own their own rickshaws.

This area falls on the outskirts of the town and is almost in the green belt. For garbage they go to the thickly populated areas of the city. Around 5 or 6 am their hunt for garbage starts. Here rickshaw comes to their rescue. Sometimes the whole family sits on the rickshaw and enjoys a ride. Whatever the weather, the family riding together keep getting down one by one as the rags mount up. Towards the end only the rickshaw and the puller are there giving company to each other. And then he too gets busy in sorting out the rags.

Mornings are better for such a venture because the

roads are clear and from a distance one can easily locate polythene, waste-paper, bottles and iron-chips. One doesn't have to brush shoulders in a crowd to pick them up. At the end of the day every rag-picker adjusts the sack of rags between his seat and that of the passenger.

Rahman is one rag-picker. After dinner he sets out again with his family in the rickshaw and they rags from the garbage tins falling on the way. Some people prefer afternoons for such a pick. Rahman is one of them.

'For a rag-picker a cart is any day better than a rickshaw. Why did you go for a rickshaw then?' Instead of him his wife replied, 'A second hand-rickshaw is cheaper and more readily available here in the city. Second hand carts are a rarity.'

Rahman added further, 'In a rickshaw you can offer a ride to your family and adjust your sack easily. There is scope for carrying passengers too which means ready money.'

handicap, having lost their jobs and some others began it with the thought of providing employment to the poor. Only 13 per cent came in this line for some other reasons.

Rickshaw-drivers carrying people on their rickshaw in lieu of money are only males. In the rural areas of Delhi one sees a few women carrying luggage in the 'thela'-rickshaws. A few women can be seen carrying load (even if junk) even on cycle-rickshaws in Ghaziabad and Faridabad. Women are on the margins even as the rickshaw-owners. These women are 1.5 and 2.3 per cent in Haryana and Uttar Pradesh while the percentage from the point of view of the entire NCR is only 1.6 per cent. Male rickshaw-owners in the region are 98.4 per cent. There are a few questions related to the rickshaw-owners, which we asked only the owners in Delhi. According to the information given by the them, most of the owners come from the peasant community. 48.6 per cent. Only 31.4 per cent have been associated traditionally the cycle-rickshaw business and 5.7 per cent owners are associated with it through shop-keeping. People associated with running the rickshaws are related to work like rickshaw-driving, running milk booths, tailoring, junk deals and other traditional work. Owners associated with these different traditional works are 2.9 per cent each. They had different goals as rickshaw-owners. 45.7 per cent have taken to rickshaw-ownership - to get fruitful employment, 25.7 per cent came to this proffession through some acquaintance, 20 per cent became rickshaw-owners due

to their being the locals and 2.9 per cent put their hands in this business in Delhi for various other reasons.

The Problem of License

Civic bodies in some places in NCR issue licenses for rickshaws. In some other places a license is not needed. A license for those rickshaws run on rent in any town is acquired by the rickshaw-owner. Though they are issued in the name of the driver but the entire fee, which includes actual license fee as well as bribe-money, is paid by the owner. He invests fully in buying or assembling the rickshaws and gives them out for rent according to his pleasure. Different owners tell different stories about this license fee. According to 21.4 per cent owners in the entire region, the license fee is between Rs. 10 and 30, 25.6 per cent put it between Rs. 30 and 60, 3.9 per cent between Rs. 60 and 100, 5.5 per cent between 100 and 150 rupees, and 11.45 peg it over Rs. 150. 1.9 per cent owners say that license is not made here 28.6 per cent owners say that for the issuance of licenses rickshaws are not being passed for now. 1.6 per cent say that they don't know anything about this rule. One can feel while talking to these owners that they are not being honest with the information. Some of them even add the bribe-money to the license fee as actual license fee. People don't get their licenses made in those towns where the rules are not enforced strictly. They keep their rickshaws running by paying officials of municipal bodies. They don't even know what the actual license fee is. It is not that they don't want to get their licenses made. They know that in the event of non-payment of bribe the officials wouldn't let the license be issued under the pretext of rules and regulations.

50.7 per cent (73 per cent in Haryana sub-region) feel that license fee is justified. Against this 48.8 per cent (62.5 per cent in the UP sub-region) consider it excessive. Only 0.5 per cent feels it is less. Since a license is not required in Rajasthan, people here, don't express any view in this regard, 84 per cent owners say that among the things needed for getting the rickshaw passed—frame number and the last passing receipt - are most important.

17.9 per cent owners in the Haryana sub-region and 2.9 per cent in the Delhi sub-region say that the name and address of the rickshaw-driver is needed for the license. No rickshaw-owner from the UP sub-region has any views in this regard, nor does he mention the ration card. But 3 per cent owners in Haryana and 11.4 per cent in the Delhi sub-regions consider a ration card necessary for license, 4.7 per cent owners say that one doesn't need any paper for the license. No owner says this in Delhi but those saying this in Haryana and UP sub-regions are 9 and 3.6 per cent respectively. There are few owners who consider all the above things necessary for license while some others mention other things. Such owners are only in Haryana where their percentage is 1.5 and 6 respectively.

The license for rickshaw is not made throughout the year in the offices of civic bodies. Because of this some rickshaw-owners cannot get licenses made for their rickshaws despite wanting to do so. Hence, 58.4 per cent owners are of the opinion that the licenses should be made throughout year just like the other vehicles. Only 43.5 per cent owners support completely abolishing the license fee though those in favour of this move in the Delhi sub-region are 51.4 per cent. On the other hand 56.5 per cent (62.5 per cent in UP sub-region) owners are in favour of a license fee. They have difference of opinion over the issue of license fee. Those in favour of abolishing the fee say that: (1) This is a means of employment for the poor. (2) It does not provide much income. (3) It is necessary to encourage rickshaws. Those professing these three opinions are 53.8, 9.7 and 14.0 per cent respectively while 22.6 per cent owners give some other reasons as well. On the other hand those supporting the license fee give these arguments: (1) Rickshaws run on the streets belonging to the government. (2) The government will suffer from the abolition of the fee. (3) There will be an unprecedented increase in the number of rickshaws. Hence it is not proper to make rickshaws license free. Those professing these three views are 41.3, 31.4 and 10.7 per cent owners respectively. 7.4 per cent owners give some other reasons in this regard. About 9.1 per cent owners want the fee to be reduced slightly.

The 'challan' of rickshaw by the civic bodies depends mainly on the town concerned. Hence, 55.2 per cent owners in Haryana and 33.9 per cent in the UP sub-regions say that the rickshaws are not 'challaned'. But among those who accept this fact 18.2 per cent talk of it being between Rs. 50 and 100, about 2 per cent between Rs. 100 and 200, about 9 per cent between Rs. 200 and 300, 6.5 per cent between Rs. 300 and 500 and 24.3 per cent have different views about the challan fee. Despite the ever-widening roads in the city and despite an increase in the number of the flyovers and underground subways the problem of traffic jams on the streets is continuously increasing. The main reason for this is an increase in the number of all kinds of vehicles. But the common perception among the administration and ordinary people is that the rickshaw is mainly responsible for traffic jams. But the rickshaw-owners don't agree with this. 9.1 per cent owners of Rajasthan sub-region and 14.3 per cent in the Delhi sub-region clearly say that rickshaws don't cause traffic jams. The culprits for the jams are heavy vehicles - 36.4 per cent owners of the region feel this way. Also, 8.1 per cent consider the auto-rickshaws, 2.6 per cent encroachment by the shopkeepers,

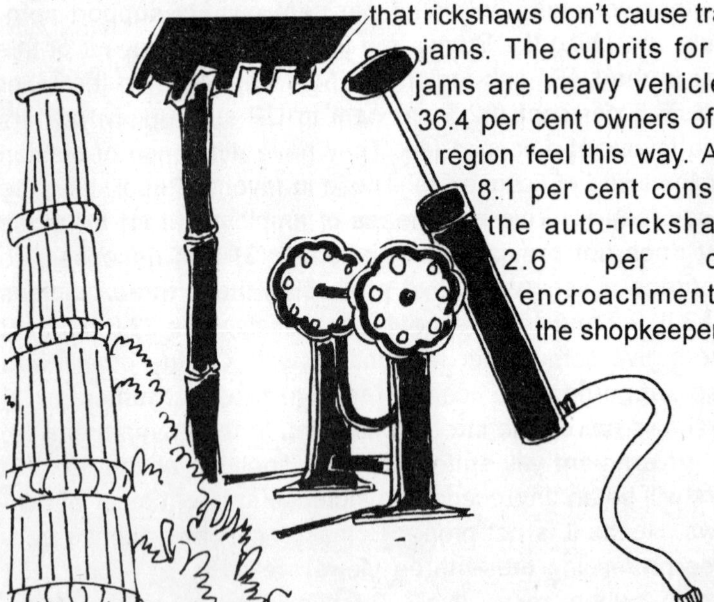

per cent bad roads, 1.3 per cent narrow roads and 1 per cent owners hold local fairs responsible for traffic jams. One per cent owners consider the lack of rickshaw-stands one of the reasons for traffic jams. At the same time 7.8 per cent owners (91 per cent in the Rajasthan sub-region) say that they don't face traffic jams in their towns. 4.2 per cent owners (17.1 per cent in Delhi) cite some other reasons for the jams.

Rickshaw Garage

A rickshaw-owner has many rickshaws. Garages are needed to keep them as well as for their maintenance and repair. There is severe lack of such spaces in the city. Hence there has to be some arrangement for these rickshaws. Those rickshaw-owners who are well off or who have their own place run their garages own and those who don't have such places of their own keep their rickshaws either on rented land or on government land (which includes vacant plots and part of streets). According to the survey, 19.5 per cent owners run their garages on their own land while 23.7 per cent on the rented

land. A big section of the owners (53.2 per cent) runs the garages on government land and 1.5 per cent rickshaw-owners in the UP sub-region use village land for the purpose. And 3.8 per cent in Haryana and 0.8 per cent rickshaws in the UP sub-region remain with their drivers. Almost 1 per cent owners in NCR keep their rickshaws in temples, schools or other such places. A majority 73.2 per cent of those using government land don't pay anything to the government or anybody else in lieu of this but 26.8 per cent do pay somebody. Most of the rickshaw-owners have only one garage, but a few of the owners own more than one garage.

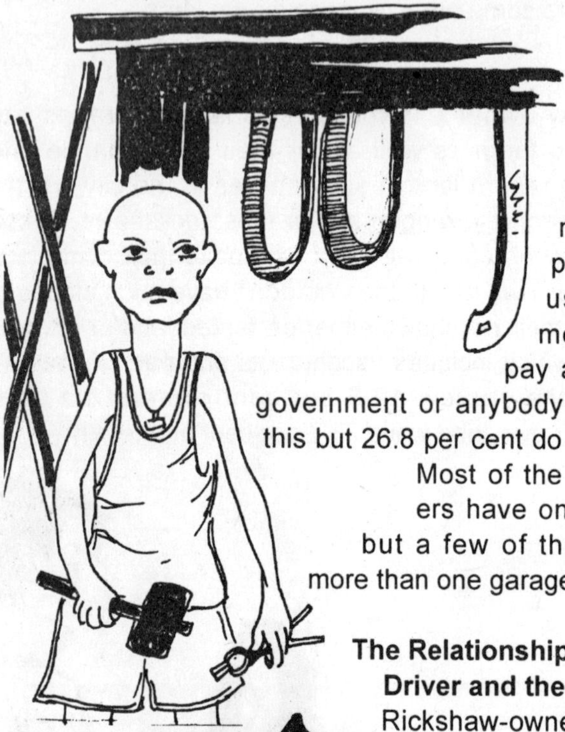

The Relationship between the Driver and the Owner

Rickshaw-owner renst out his rickshaw to only those about whom he/she is sure that they wouldn't make any trouble in paying rent and will keep the rickshaw safe. Hence, 96 per cent owners give their rickshaws only on the basis of security and 4 per cent sometimes do rent out without any security. Moreover, 99.3 per cent owners accept this security on a personal basis. Hence

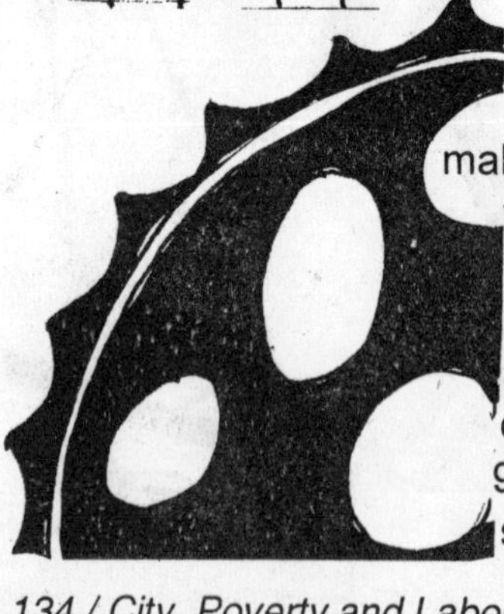

if any acquaintance of the rickshaw-owner accepts the responsibility for the driver then the owner rents out his rickshaw to him. With this establishment of a bond between the driver and the owner, the latter remains ready to help the former with 92.5 per cent owners saying that if their rickshaw-driver falls sick then they help him out.

The owner gets attached to the driver thanks to the rickshaw. But not all owners have the same attitude towards the drivers. They behave differently vis-à-vis weekly holiday for the drivers. Forty-two percent owners give concession in the rent only when the rickshaw-drivers deposit their rickshaws in the garage, 26.6 per cent don't charge the rent for the off day. 14.6 per cent owners give four off days in a month, 4.2 per cent owners waive off the rent only when the driver is continuously driving their rickshaw, 1.6 per cent owners don't take the rent for one day from those rickshaw-drivers who submit their rent regularly and 3.6 per cent owners charge half rent for that day. Some owners totally give it off during emergencies. Some gives rickshaw-drivers no rest at all, while some others charge rent even for off days from new drivers.

The owners behave differently in the event of the rickshaw-driver losing the rickshaw. 18.2 per cent owners sit with the rickshaw-driver to decide about it, 50 per cent owners charge half the price of the rickshaw from the rickshaw-drivers and 2.6 per cent charge the full cost. However, 9.4 per cent owners claim that most of the rickshaw-drivers don't return anything at all, 13.3 per cent owners don't do anything, 4.2 per cent go out in search of the rickshaw themselves. About 2 per cent owners say that they have never lost their rickshaw.

If the rickshaw doesn't bring money then no owner will want to give the rickshaw on rent. It is true that due to their various problems most of the rickshaw-drivers don't pay the rent on time - 88.6 per cent owners complain about this. Only 11.4 per cent owners get their rent on time.

65.9 per cent owners charge a rent between Rs. 10-15 per day, 31.8 per cent between Rs. 15-20 and 2.3 per cent between Rs 20-25 per day. The rent of any rickshaw depends upon the locality and condition of the rickshaw.

While the rent is high in Delhi, it is low in towns like Sohna and Hodal. Old rickshaw is available on low rent compared to the new one—this holds true for almost all the cities. Which person holds how many rickshaws depend upon his/her economic condition and the size of the town.

Big owners are found more in geographically and numerically bigger cities compared to the smaller ones. Yet, whatever the city, owners with better economic status remain influential, but their economic status can't be seen as indicative of absolute prosperity but rather of comparatively having a little more money. There are people who own between 2 to 500 rickshaws in NCR. From what the rickshaw-owners have accepted themselves, 51 per cent own between 2 to 20 rickshaw, 14.6 per cent between 21 to 30, 11.7 per cent between 31 to 40, 7.8 per cent between 41 to 50, 2.3 per cent between 100 to 200 rickshaws and 0.6 per cent own over 200. Rickshaw-owners don't give exact details of the rickshaws owned by them, as they fear something untoward will happen if they do.

Each rickshaw-owner hires many rickshaw-drivers. These rickshaw-drivers are of different age. They comprise minors, young, older and all kinds of people. 2.9 per cent owners have rickshaw-drivers below 18 years of age while about 97 per cent owners have rickshaw-drivers between 18 to 30 years. Similarly, about 28 per cent owners have rickshaw-drivers between 31-40 years among the eldest while 72 per cent have people over 40 years driving rickshaws for them.

The World of Rickshaw-mechanics

The world of rickshaw-mechanics is as diverse as that of rickshaw-owners and drivers. One mechanic is different from the other with respect to age, caste, religion, original place, educational qualification, income and traditional work of the family etc. However, Hundreds of mechanics might look alike despite these differences. They might be different caste-wise yet be the same religion-wise. Some of them might be same in age but different in terms of their incomes. Among those with the same education one might be married while the other might not be. Among the married ones, one is a Hindu while the other is a Sikh. Like a riddle this complex process continues among the mechanics through which one doesn't even realise when one mechanic comes into the class of the other and when he/she moves away to be part of another. But one gets some clear indications from the data and facts available on the basis of conversatiosn with them. This information help in resolving this knot.

Most mechanics in NCR belong to the 18-30 years age group (about 47 per cent). After this come those between 31-40 years (27 per cent). Then come those in the bracket of 41 years and above—21.7 per cent. 4.2 per cent mechanics are below 18 years. It is indeed noticeable that in the Delhi and Rajasthan sub-regions neither owners nor mechanics are below 18 years. The caste-wise break up of rickshaw mechanics in the region is : scheduled castes (22.2 per cent), scheduled tribes (0.5 per cent), other backward castes (24.3 per cent), high caste (30.7 per cent). 20.6 per cent mechanics refused to reveal their caste and 1.6 per cent said that they did not believe in its. The percentage of scheduled tribes in Haryana is 1.3 per cent most of the mechanics are Hindus like the owners and drivers. Their percentage is 62.4. Mechanics from the Muslim community are 31.2 per cent. Those professing Sikh and Christian religion are 5.8 and 0.5 per cent respectively. One couldn't find Christian mechanics in Rajasthan, U.P. and Delhi and Sikh mechanics in Delhi and UP.

Maximum number of mechanics are high school pass (27 per cent). Almost an equal number are illiterates (26.5 per cent). Middle school pass mechanics are 20.1 per cent and literate are 13.8 per cent. 10.6 per cent mechanics have acquired primary education. Intermediate pass and graduate rickshaw mechanics are about 2 per cent.

These mechanics have come from different parts of the country. Some of them have permanently settled in this city while some others still retain their linkages with their native places. They keep going back there every six-months or every year or according to the need. Most of the mechanics come from U.P. in NCR (49.2 per cent). They are mostly in the UP sub-region (89.6 per cent). They are 45.8 per cent in Delhi sub-region and in Haryana sub-region 16.7 per cent. They are not to be found in Rajasthan. Haryanvi mechanics come second in the entire region—26.5 per cent. They are more in the Haryana sub-region—57.7 per cent. They are present in other sub-regions as well but not in significant enough numbers. They are only 20 per cent in Rajasthan, 8.3 per cent in Delhi and only 1.3 per cent in U.P. sub-regions. Bihari mechanics are the third largest in the region-12.7 per cent. They are present in Haryana, UP, Rajasthan and Delhi. Rajasthani mechanics are mostly in the Rajasthan sub-region (70 per cent). They are also present in Haryana and Delhi sub-regions. It is an interesting fact that UP mechanics are not to be found in Rajasthan sub-region and those from the latter are not found in the UP sub-region. Bengali mechanics are present in the Haryana and U.P. sub-regions. Mechanics are also from other parts of the country in the NCR. They constitute 4.2 per cent.

Traditional occupation of the families of these mechanics are diverse. Only 20.6 per cent come from the traditional occupation of cycle and rickshaw repair in the entire region. Most mechanics (37.6 per cent) come from labouring families, 19.6 per cent come from farming background and 6.3 per cent from service. Rickshaw mechanics also come from families associated with professions like vending, barber, shoemaker, tailor, goldsmith, potter etc. Almost 7 per cent also come from the families associated with running shops and rickshaw-driving. It can be said that the mechanics can be associated with families coming from all kinds of traditional professions. The difference in their percentage is another matter.

All mechanics working in the cities don't have a similar residence system. They all have different problems in this regard. 60.8 per cent mechanics live in their own houses in the entire NCR—whether they live in the cities or go back to their villages after day's work, 22.2 per cent live in rented rooms while 0.5 per cent in rented hutments (4.2 per cent in Delhi). Those living in their own hutments are 7.4 per cent (29.2 per cent in Delhi). 6.3 per cent (25 per cent in Delhi) live in the rickshaw garages, a little more than 1 per cent spend their nights at their friends' or relations' places and 0.5 per cent on the footpath. Almost 1 per cent have made some other arrangement for their stay. 68.3 per cent mechanics started their work as cycle and rickshaw mechanics after coming to NCR. Others did some other work in the beginning and later became rickshaw-mechanic - 4.2 per cent were rickshaw-drivers earlier, 7.9 per cent started as factory labourers, 8.5 per cent as daily wage labourers, 1.1 per cent as assistants in shops, 2.1 per cent as car mechanics, 1.1 per cent through white washing houses, 2.1 per cent as shopkeepers, 0.5 per cent as helpers in buses, 1.1 per cent as tea shop owners and 3 per cent as carpenters, vegetable sellers, book binders, drivers, and milk sellers etc. But due to change in their conditions because of one or the other reason they were forced to change their professions.

Some have come to this profession only recently while some others have been there for years. 1.6 per cent have been mechanics for less than a year, 23.8 per cent between 1 to 5 years, 28.6 per cent between 5 to 10 years, 30.7 per cent between 10 to 20 years, 13.2 per cent between 20 to 40 years and 2.1 per cent have been working for more than 40 years. They all have their reasons or compulsions behind this work. While 10.6 per cent claim that they came into this profession because they couldn't find any other work. 8.5 per cent claim to be in it since childhood. On the other hand 13.2 per cent term it as their familial work, 53.4 per cent have chosen this work for employment and 14.3 per cent say that they chose this work because with little capital one's own business can be established.

The life of a rickshaw-mechanic is quite tough. the labours or is forced to labour according to his conditions. 5.3 per cent mechanics labour for less than 8 hours, 87.8 per cent between 8 and 12 hours and 6.9 per cent work between 12 and 16 hours everyday. At the same time 1.1 per cent mechanics work for less than 6 months in a year, 19.6 per cent over 6 months but less than a year and 79.4 per cent work throughout the year. Those who don't work throughout the year work in fields, in brick-kiln factories, work with the contractor to cook food for marriages etc. The reason for this is that they earn more through these jobs as compared to what they earn as mechanic.

These mechanics have to labour a lot. Many of them also find it very monotonous. They need some kind of entertainment but they all don't have such means available to them. 12.7 per cent mechanics listen to the radio while 27 per cent watch television. 1.1 per cent also watch cinema sometimes and 11.6 per cent fulfill this need of relaxation by talking to their friends. A small member 0.5 per cent read newspapers and 47.1 per cent mechanics like to spend their moments of entertainment as relaxation.

Mechanics of the region fall sick once in a while. Some of them (9.5 per cent) get treated at the government hospitals and some others (7.4 per cent) take medicines as per the advice of the chemist at the medicine shop.and 1.1 per cent take recourse to the home remedies. But a large section goes to private medical shops and health centres. Their percentage is about 79.4 per cent. 2.6 per cent mechanics say that they never fall sick. Meanwhile in the event of sickness 92.6 per cent mechanics get themselves treated with their own saved money while the rest 7.4 per cent borrow it from their friends and relatives.

These rickshaw mechanics belong to different levels in

terms of their skills. Most of them (77.2 per cent) have learnt this work from their fathers, brothers or under some other mechanic but 22.8 per cent have learnt it on their own through regular practice. Out of those working in NCR (barring Delhi), 30.9 per cent say that there was somebody else in this profession from the family, while 69.1 per cent say that they were the only ones in this profession in the family.

All the mechanics all over the region say that one didn't need a license to become a mechanic. More then half 55.9 per cent mechanics in the region said that a friend or a relative introduced them to a rickshaw-garage owner, while 44.1 per cent contacted the owners themselves of all the mechanics. 8.5 per cent get their payment daily, while 91.5 per cent get it as monthly salary. The garage owners have a different attitude towards weekly holidays. 23.7 per cent don't get this kind of off day, while 74.6 per cent do get it. Some others (1.7 per cent) don't get it uniformly. Sometimes the mechanic doesn't turn up due to some reason. In such an eventuality, 30.5 per cent say that their salary is cut but 69.5 per cent owners don't do such a thing.

A majority 67.8 per cent also say that the owners help them during days of illness, while 32.2 per cent say they don't get any help from the owners. Those who get help, get it in different forms. Out of these 80 per cent accept that the owners help them during the days of illness. This help they get as an advance which is later deducted from their salaries, 2.5 per cent owners grant just leave. But there are 17.5 per cent owners who help in various ways besides giving economic help and granting leave. Mechanics working in a garage have basically two kinds of mindset. Almost 70 per cent of them dream of owning their own garage so that they can increase their income besides having absolute freedom. But the other 30.5 per cent find it better to continue working in the garage. This is because they find running their own garage burdensome apart from having money crunch. Those who want to open their own garage and have not been able to do so are because they have not been able to acquire requisite capital - 92.7 per cent

The Rickshaw-riders: Some Snaps

Occasional tiffs, but inter-dependence

Rickshaw-drivers are divided on the point of going for fixed passengers: 1.2 per cent of them call it a source of fixed income, 1 per cent of them look up to them as a source of loan in duress, 3.8 per cent of them call it convenient because it saves them from loitering all around in search of passengers and 9 per cent of them have not given iy a thought to it. while 34.4 per cent of them refuse to call it advantageous 50.6 per cent of them do find it beneficial. Getting a regular amount monthly helps them plan in advance for future investments. This 'fat' amount could be anything between Rs. 50 to Rs. 4000. Survey-data tells us that from fixed passengers 28 per cent of the rickshaw-drivers earn Rs. 50-500, 32.2 per cent Rs. 500-1000, 28.8 per cent Rs. 1000-2000 and 11 per cent

Rs. 2000-4000. Rickshaw-drivers treat rickshaws as a source of income but they also, like all wage earners, are not devoid of human sentiments. Two third of them reported that at some point or the other they have carried an old man or a sick one, a woman or a child in distress—free of cost. Getting an address wrong or taking a different route gives rise to tiffs too, but 53 per cent of the rickshaw-drivers find the passengers well-behaved, 4.4 per cent of them find them atrocious and 42.5 per cent of them think that it varies. Very few cities have a fixed fare list. Generally the fare is a subject of negotiation. It varies according to the distance, the number of passengers, luggage items, the gradation of the city, the time taken, weather-conditions and the condition of roads etc. It can be anything between Rs. 2 to Rs. 25. Many passengers do not settle the fare in the beginning and hand over any amount at the end of the ride. Some quote lesser distance and some go beyond the point quoted. This naturally leads to a minor tiff.

Once or Again and Again: They All Ride

Rickshaw-drivers in Delhi have passengers from the entire world —not only Delhi-wallahs but tourists also fancy a rickshaw-ride especially for small distances—a tourist spot, a cinema hall, station or a bus-stand. People from different walks of life and all age groups love a rickshaw-ride—artists, businessmen, teachers, students, lawyers and office-goers—occasionally opt for a rickshaw. Inaugurating the modern rickshaw, Sheila Dixit also enjoyed a rickshaw-ride. Her inaugural speech called it eco-friendly. 'As it consumes no fuel, it also helps us save foreign currency.'

As Long As We Are Hungry and Deprived

Panipat manufactures blankets, woolen sheets and durees etc. that are loaded on to rickshaws for transportation. Some rickshaw-drivers carry ropes with them to help out the transporters. Neatly they tie the load so that it doesn't fall off. Often they overload in the hope of more money. Gopal Singh, 38, travels on loaded rickshaws. He reports, 'Sometimes children and old men are also dragged in to this profession. This tells upon their life and health.' Comrade Ramdatta reports, 'People in our country work not according to their flair and aptitude, they do not work for betterment but to ends meet. Rickshaw-driving is not considered respectable in our country, still lakhs of them pull rickshaw for the lack of better avenues!'

A Human Bondage At least

Jyotsna, 29, a housewife in Ghaziabad, says, 'They must be given due wages and at no price should they be overloaded the way they are—4-5 adults on one rickshaw is a common sight! And when it comes to paying them, they take out the least of the change they are carrying in their pocket. All this is highly objectionable... They deserve very humane treatment. If they come all the way to drop us home, they should be served water and snacks." Satbeer Sharma, 48, observes, 'Many of the rickshaw-drivers sleep on footpaths—roughing out in the worst weather. The government must provide them shelters—absolutely free of cost.'

A Cycle After All

Old Mr. K. K. Khanna, industrialist, reports, 'Rickshaws have been in Meerut since 1948. My own paternal house was at a place 20 miles towards the west of Lahore. Till 1946 I was totally ignorant of what a rickshaw looked like. The tales of rickshaws plying on Delhi roads kept us excited. When we migrated, I saw rickshaw for the first time, but that was not an exciting experience. A man pulling another man was not a good sight. For 4-6 months I couldn't muster the courage to board rickshaw. Some of my friends still find it cruel... Gradually, somehow I pepped myself up thinking don't I sit at the back of a friend's bicycle? A rickshaw is a cycle after all." Then he compares the Meerut rickshaws to the rickshaws in Bihar, "Rickshaws in Patna are grand: high and broad enough to accommodate more than two people. Rickshaws here are narrow and low and there is no protection from the sun, the dust and dirt and the rain.'

The Youth Ahead

In Delhi the percentage of passengers less than 18 of age is 14.5 and that of the age group 18-30 is 46.2; 18.6 per cent of them fall in the age group 31-40 and 20.8 per cent of them are above 41 years of age. 27.4 per cent of them are women and 72.6 per cent of them men. The percentage of women passengers less than 18 years of age is 7 per cent and that of women between 18-30 is 54 per cent. 10.3 per cent of the women passengers fall in the age group of 31-40 and 17.2 per cent of them are more than 41 years old. Male passengers who are 18 years 13 per cent, for 18-30 years this percentage is 43.3, for 31-40 this figure is 21.6 per cent and for more then 41 years it is 22.1 per cent. Highest age in male category has the percentage of 22.1. These figures stand out against the common notion that children, women and old men prefer a rickshaw. The youth are the most mobile for various reasons; it boards rickshaws too in largest numbers.

A Few Suggestions in Favour of Rickshaw-drivers

A quarter (25.2 per cent) of the passengers advised social security—the education of kids, health insurance, security of life and goods and life-insurance etc. 3.1 per cent said that they must be sensitised against drinking, gambling and drug-addition, 12.3 per cent of the passengers appealed for infra-structural supports like a separate stand and a separate parking, a separate lane and a decent night-halt with proper toilet facilities, 13.8 per cent laid emphasis on a fixed rate list, pension-facilities and alternative livelihood for the old and the weak, 18.9 per cent of them expressed their social concern and suggested that riding rickshaws should be popularised to keep rickshaw-wallahs in workable financial health, 7.9 per cent passengers offered advise to popularise rickshaws as the only eco-friendly vehicle and 18.9 per cent gave other kinds of miscellaneous suggestions to improve the life conditions of rickshaw-drivers.

Democracy: Where is this?

Off and on these rickshaw-drivers are beaten black and blue. Confiscation and deliberate puncturing of tyres for the slightest violation of rules are rampant too. According to a rider, the remedy for this deplorable situation can only be the united struggle of everybody who happens to be related to this profession. Another rider explains, 'After the PM's notification a rickshaw ride in Delhi has become all the more cumbersome. The whole of the city has been divided into red, yellow and green areas. Rickshaws can ply only in the green area, which is so small...

Between two green areas, lies a red area where rickshaws can't ply... Frequent change of rickshaws makes the ride expensive. And if the rickshaw-driver dares transgressing, the police punctures his tyres. This upsets the passenger and he is made to feel that the country runs according to the convenience of the car-wallas. Who cares for the rickshaw and rickshaw-drivers? Passengers, mechanics and owners should also join hands in struggling against the odds that these rickshaw-drivers have to face.'

mechanics say this. 4.9 per cent have been unable to open the garage due to lack of space. 2.4 per cent have been postponing their plans of opening the garage because they feel they are not yet ready for it.

Which mechanic earns how much depends a lot on the place where he works. A rickshaw-mechanic usually doubles up as a cycle-mechanic as well. Hence those working at the site also earn from this work. Normally those mechanics who put up their stalls near offices, schools, hospitals and local markets etc. tend to earn more. But if the number of mechanics increases in proportion to the rickshaws and bicycles in the area then their earnings tend to go down. 20 per cent mechanics earn between Rs. 20-60 per day, 55.4 per cent between Rs. 60-100, 23.1 per cent between Rs. 100-150 and 1.5 per cent earn over Rs. 200. They spend this money everyday on their accommodation, food, tea, snacks, and other purchases 23.1 per cent mechanics say that they cannot save anything, 17.7 per cent save between Rs. 10-30, 30 per cent between Rs. 30-50, 26.9 per cent between Rs. 50-100 and 2.3 per cent save over Rs. 100 daily.

They spend the saved money according to their needs. 86 per cent say that they spend it on their families, 9 per cent send it to their homes, 4 per cent keep it safe while 1 per cent spend it on themselve.

That shop runs better which remains closed only once in a while. If any shop remains open daily then its income increases. Most of the mechanics say that the day they are not in a position to open the shop, they can't find a replacement. There are about 80 per cent who say thus. Only 20 per cent mechanics have some replacement for them who is usually a relative or a friend who has the required skills.

We asked Delhi rickshaw-mechanics since how long they had been in Delhi and 8.3 per cent said that they were here for duration between 1-6 months, 12.5 per cent between 1-5 years, 16.7 per cent between 10-15 years and 16.7 per cent said they had based in Delhi for over 20 years. We also asked them about the reason behind their coming to Delhi and 70.8

per cent mentioned employment, and 8.3 per cent mentioned other reasons.

The relationship between rickshaw-drivers and passengers

The rickshaw has no importance without the driver and the passenger riding on it. These three always go together and share a bittersweet relation with each other. They fight among each other and yet it is the rickshaw-driver who carries any hassled passenger even in case he/she has no money. However, it is not a strange thing to see them fight over non-payment of agreed money or taking the rickshaw further than pre-agreed destination and 23.9 per cent passengers agreed that they have fought over this issue. Yet 76.1 per cent passengers denied having fought over any such issue. There are moments when a rickshaw-driver leaves an indelible mark with his behaviour. - 30.8 per cent passengers recounted some incident in which they remembered a particular rickshaw-driver but 69.2 per cent could not recall any such incident.

There is diversity as well as similarity among passengers in terms of age, sex, religion and caste etc. There is also a lot of difference as well as similarity in their destination and travel routes. There are sufficient elements of similarity as well as difference in terms of height and complexion among the passengers. The same can be observed in their thinking and behaviour. Passengers have different opinions about ecology, democracy on the roads, transport system, change in the model of the rickshaw and the lives of rickshaw-drivers. The facts and data accumulated from discussions with passengers relating to the rickshaw helped in giving answers to many questions related to the rickshaw-drivers.

Only 16.4 per cent of them are daily users of the rickshaw while 83.6 per cent of them are occasional users. Rickshaws link them with bus-stands, railway statiosn, offices, bazaars, schools-colleges and fair-grounds. In the National Capital Region 17.9 per cent riders use rickshaws for bus-stands and railway stations, 8.2 per cent for offices, 57.2 per cent for bazaar, 12.3 per cent for schools-colleges and 4.4 per cent for other sites (such as hospitals).

Rickshaw riders are aware and alert. They talk openly about the gains of a rickshaw ride. Of them 22 per cent consider rickshaw a means of employment, 33 per cent of them find it convenient, 13.8 per cent of them are of the opinion that rickshaws are eco-friendly, 31.1 per cent of them think that the rickshaw serves these three purposes. For short distances 94.3 per cent of the people vouch for rickshaws, 3.8 per cent for three-wheelers and 1.9 per cent for buses.

Amidst the fast moving motor driven vehicles, a rickshaw-rider sits glued to his seat—scared and apprehensive of being knocked down. Only 6.9 per cent of the riders feel that there should not be a separate lane on the road for cycles and rickshaws. The remaining 93.1 per cent are strongly in favour of a separate lane.

In the narrowest of lanes a rickshaw makes way without blocking traffic, 75.2 per cent of the riders are in favour of a ban against the entry of heavy vehicles in narrow lanes. 21.4 per cent of the passengers want this ban on tempos and three-wheelers, 1.6 per cent a ban on 'buggi' and hand-carts and 1.9 per cent are against the entry of even a rickshaw in a narrow lane.

A majority 97.2 per cent passengers feel that encouraging rickshaw-rides would contribute a lot to pollution-check. With the steep population rise in the metro cities massive traffic jams are a major problem for which 62.9 per cent passengers hold car, bus and trucks responsible, 2.2 per cent put the blame on 'buggi' and 'tonga', 27 per cent on tempo and three-wheelers, 1.3 per cent on motorcycles, 3.1 per cent on rickshaws and 3.5 per cent on cycle, hand-carts etc.

Should there be a ban on the rickshaw? 41.8 per cent of the passengers oppose this, 18.9 per cent think that such a ban will result in the rise of unemployment, 24.2 per cent want to encourage it for pollution control, 5.7 per cent want to encourage rickshaws as a source of employment generation and 1.3 per cent came up with suggestions on how the rickahaw-business can avoid this ban.

On the other hand 12.6 per cent passengers consider a rickshaw-ride unsafe, but unlike them 87.4 per cent think it quite safe.

Among rickshow users, 19.5 per cent passengers had seen the new model of the rickshaw, 16.7 per cent of them had just heard about it, 61.3 per cent were completely ignorant about it, and 2.5 per cent of them claimed that they had ridden on the good looking 'new' rickshaw.

In case of even a minor lapse, the MCD destroys rickshaws and 94.4 per cent of the passengers call this unjustified, and the remaining 5.6 per cent think that they do deserve this kind of treatment.

The majority however are in favour of rickshaws and rickshaw-drivers.

Conclusions

In the NCR areas of Delhi the quadrangular of rickshaw-drivers, rickshaw-riders, rickshaw-mechanics and rickshaw-owners is not a square but an rectangle. On the long arms of the rectangle rest the rickshaw-drivers and rickshaw-riders. On the smaller arms are rickshaw-owners and rickshaw-mechanics. Surrounded by the four arms, life is moving at various paces. The globalised modernisation wants to break this rectangle but in vain. Circumstances in Asia differ from those in Europe. the urbanization of India is not comparable to that of city-states of Singapore and Hong-Kong. Obviously not only in near but also in the distant future we can't even visualize an Indian city without rickshaws. The close study of the relationship of the city with poverty and labour brings us to some conclusions. These conclusions can lay the foundation of future policies, that humanise, equalize and democratise these relationships.

Living standards and life styles of rickshaw-drivers depend on their economic, social and cultural background. They take pride in physical labour and are not shy of it. They are mostly addicted to tobacco, bidi and 'gutka'. Only a few among them can afford liquor and smack etc. Unions exist only in name and instead of sensitising them they keep them demoralised and demotivated. Their real interest lies in collecting funds for 'Bhagwati Jagrans'. With a little encouragement, rickshaws can help us in fighting unemployment, pollution, derth of petroleum-fuel and encourage a cheap and convenient means of transport. This can also enable us to save foreign currency which can be diverted to other schemes of development. The technique of the rickshaw needs a face-lift, but rickshaw-drivers can make the best of these only when all rickshaws earn both legitimacy and government support. Otherwise the new rickshaw will also suffer the fate of the modern rickshaw

The tussle between a rickshaw-driver and rickshaw-owner ultimately goes against rickshaw-driver. A co-operative society of the rickshaw-drivers could be a positive step in their upliftment. Educating and acquainting them with all traffic rules of the traffic can easily bring down the rate of accidents. In any case, damaging a rickshaw amounts to robbery, a deprivation of the total capital he can lay his claim on. This is against the basic right of equality granted to all citizens of India. Throwing a self-employed person out of employment is both a sin and a crime. The ratio of rickshaw and other modes of transport in a city should be ascertained keeping the common citizens' needs in mind. Letting motor vehicles grow out of proportion is a real national waste and this results in nothing more than messy traffic jams.

Rickshaw-drivers and rickshaw-mechanics are mostly first generation migrant poor struggling for basic amenities of like water, electricity, fuel, latrine and a roof over their head. - 48.6 per cent of these rickshaw-drivers and one fourth of the rickshaw mechanics are illiterate. One-fourth of the mechanics have studied till high school. Those who have shops of their own are slightly well-off, the ones working on the footpath are no better than rickshaw-drivers. Very few of them came here on their own. Most of them had relatives or friends working here when they migrated.

All rickshaw-drivers are male. Fifty per cent of them belong to the age group of 18-30 years. They adhere to different caste-groups and religions with 41 per cent of them being

OBC and three-fourth of them Hindus. Like drivers 47 per cent of the mechanics also belong to the age group of 18-30 years. 30.7 per cent of them belong to the upper castes and 24.3 per cent to OBC. 62.4 per cent of them are Hindus. Three-fourth of the rickshaw-drivers are married but they stay single with a view to saving as much for their family as possible. They live in a group to minimize on expenses and also to raise a support system against emergencies. Three-fourth of the mechanics are married and most of them live with their families. They send their kids to school (63.6 per cent). In this respect they are closer to rickshaw-owners. 49.2 per cent of them are from U.P., 26.5 per cent from Haryana and 12.7 per cent from Bihar.

Only a few of rickshaw-drivers own rickshaws. Reasons for not owning a rickshaw of their own could be paucity of fund, lack of space for keeping a rickshaw, discouragement from municipal employees and makeshift arrangement in cities. The government does not provide a loans, insurance, housing, parking and stands nor for their health and education. These basic amenities are a must for their mental and material security and also for their empowerment. Only one-fifth of the mechanics come from the families of mechanics. 37.6 per cent of the mechanics are from the family of labourers. Most of them work for eight to 20 hours day for raising enough money to support their families. Still, one-fifth of them are underemployed. During the lean period they take up some other works.

If need be they visit private health centres and during confinement rickshaw-owners help them out by providing for their treatment and giving them loans.

Most of the mechanics are trained either by friends or by relatives and they dream of running a garage of their own. But for lack of money, space and experience the dream is seldom translated into reality. The temporary lean-to shops on footpaths are often knocked down either by the Municipal Corporation or by anti-social elements. Because they do not have a union of their own, they are usually taken for a ride. Occasional training should also be provided to add to their technical know-how and enhance their efficiency levels.

Despite a definite contribution of the rickshaw to the transport system, transport policies are blind to its needs and demands. They don't even have a separate lane. Licence hassles have slashed down the number of rickshaws on the roads and many a line of control and 'lakshman-rekhas' tell upon their free movement. Rickshaws are often confiscated and damaged by the corporation official for lack of licences and by traffic Police for the slightest negligence in observing traffic rules. Both the police and the goondas take turns in harassing them, extorting money and beating them black and blue.

Male rickshaw-riders are two and a half times more than women passengers. Two-third of them fall in the age-group of 18-40 years, 83.6 per cent of them ride rickshaws off and on. They use rickshaws primarily for reaching places like bus-stops, railway stations, offices, markets, schools and collages and hospitals, etc. Most of the riders maintains that the rickshaw generates employment, helps in environmental preservation and facilitates the transport system. Riders feel scared of speedy cars or two and three wheelers. That is precisely why they suggest separate lanes for rickshaws, which can even help in removing the chronic problem of traffic jams.

Haggling and occasional tiffs are commonplace but many passengers nurse tender memories where a rickshaw-wallah came to their rescue in an emergency. For the security and protection of the passenger some rickshaw-drivers have even laid down their lives. In case of an accident they take the injured to hospitals free of cost. Sometimes they don't even demand money from those who can't pay. The socio-cultural background of the passengers also determines the nature of this relationship between the rickshaw-puller and the passenger.

Compared to the mechanics and rickshaw-drivers, rickshaw-owners are slightly better off. In the eyes of the law their profession is absolutely illegal. Still they have the chains of 200 t0 500 rickshaws under their command. For running this business they have to grease the palms of many a government officer. Therefore single rickshaw-ownership should be replaced by multiple rickshaw-ownership. This would serve the interest of both the owners and the drivers.

Most of the owners have a house, a 'jhuggi' or a room of their own. Most of them are married and stay there with their families. Some have taken it on as a family business, some have risen from the level of a rickshaw-puller or a rickshaw-mechanic. Most of them are men. One or two women rickshaw-owners are on the scene but they don't have a long chain of rickshaws. Hardly any of the owners would be below 18 years. Most of them are above 30 years, 46.1 per cent of them are Hindus and 58.1 per cent belong to the higher castes. Most of their kids go to school but very few (3.5 per cent) of them have working wives.

The highest number of ricksahw-owners hail from UP. Then come the owners from Haryana and Bihar. Their percentage is 47.1, 26.6 and 15.6 respectively. One-fourth of them are illiterate. Some of them have passed high school.

New transport policies must not be oblivious to the needs and demands of people in the rickshaw industry. Drivers, owners, mechanics and producers must have due representation in policy-framing. There should be a rickshaw network in each neighbourhood. There should be a proper rickshaw stand close to every bus-stop, railway station, marketplace and hospital etc.

There are 6677 village and 94 urban localities in the MCD area of Delhi. Peasants in villages had to give their land at throw away prices to MCD and no compensations were made. Driven out of their land—they don't have many jobs- options. Industries are also closing down rapidly and they are being thrown out of jobs. On the other hand city roads are replete with private cars and public transport. Eco-friendly buses are too costly for an average man on roads, and rickshaws have literally been pushed to the margins. For animal-driven carts too there is absolutely no space on Delhi roads.

Despite the heavy rush of vehicles on the roads, the common man is not yet a part of an integrated transport system. Well-off families are still using more than one car. Different areas of the city are not properly linked with buses. The answer to this mess is not only the broadening of roads and the building of overbridges. In fact, these measures are not even eco-friendly. The problem of traffic jams can't be resolved in this manner. A well-planned transport policy is a must. To make it pro-people only a fixed number of essential vehicles must be allowed to ply on the roads.The amount of diesel, petrol and CNG wasted in the everyday traffic jams is a national waste. If traffic jams are taken care of, lots of money can be saved and diverted towards the creation of new job opportunities.

Scientific and technical experts should also work towards improving the technology to minimise the labour of rickshaw-drivers and other pullers animals in the transport industry. Development of a city actually means the development of the poor and the under-employed. The poor are not the garbage to be thrown out of the city. They also deserve infrastructural support of a decent living. They also have the right to live and look up. National resources should all be turned towards them. In fact an integrated transport policy should be planned on the basis of available national resources. Undue importance to foreign resources will not be in the interest of the nation.

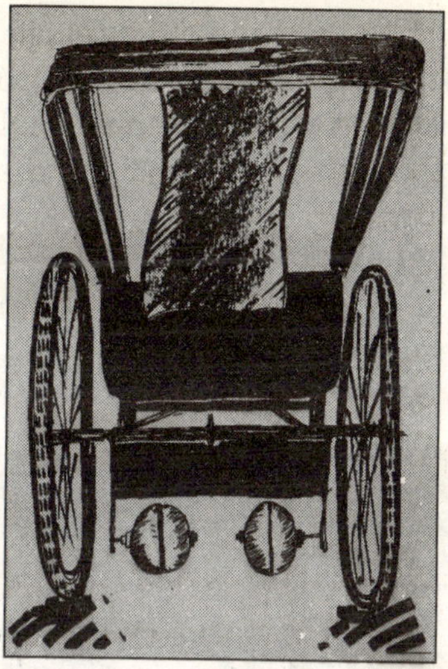

TWO

Identity and Struggle

Law, Organisation and Technology

Enmeshed in the triangle of urbanistion, poverty and labour, a study of the rickshaw and lives dependent on it clearly brings certain things to the fore. First, this urban poor, whether he came from some other village or city, was equally poverty-stricken even in his original dwelling. Second, he moved to the capital or to some other neighbouring area only because all other means of earning a livelihood had been exhausted.

Third, the policies of globalisation and liberalisation are pushing this poor man back to the same place from where he courageously ventured out to stand on his feet. Fourth, in this entire process he feels cheated and holds the government responsible for his fate.

The question which needs to be asked is that given the current state of affairs, how can a rickshaw-driver establish his identity in a huge city like Delhi? Amidst contradictory situations, which forms of organisation and struggle can benefit him in his fight for recognition. In this chapter an attempt has been made in two parts to seek answers to such queries. The first part deals with city life and the question of identity and also explores the

realities associated with it.

It describes how the absence of legal and civic recognition has made the life of a rickshaw-driver extremely miserable. And this is happening despite the fact that top-most government officials who, on the one hand, claim that the very sight of a rickshaw is an undesired aspect of a modern lifestyle, also realize its usefulness and are therefore hesitant to ban it. This section also discusses the issue of a rickshaw-driver's efforts to search for his political and socio-economic individuality. Moreover, it investigates how the difficulties of an unstable life of a rickshaw-driver snatches all means of struggle from him—a struggle, as the chapter suggests, that is vital for his existence. The second part discusses issues related to production, manufacturing and technology.

I
Destruction, Devastation and Marginalisation

These days work on the Metro Rail is being carried out on Delhi's Mall Road with great gusto. There used to be a 'basti' here—not a beautiful one but bountiful enough for thousands of its inhabitants who lived happily and earned their bread. Some did small jobs while others were street-vendors and hawkers. But this slum was sacrificed in the name of Metro Rail. It was destroyed and its residents were dumped in Metro Vihar's 'Holambi Kalan' area. Some families got a piece of land only as big as 18 sq. ft. or 12.5 sq. ft. It was here that the study group of Jan Parivahan Panchayat met a woman who was preparing food at 5 O'clock in the evening. According to her, food could not be cooked in the morning as there was nothing in the house. 'Today I felt we have not been settled but that we have been uprooted. My family was very happy in the slum at Mall Road. During our 8-10 years of stay in Delhi we had never seen such a bad day. Back at Mall Road, we had our own 'jhuggi' and rickshaw. My husband pulled the rickshaw and I worked in a 'kothi'. Both of us managed to save a little money. Our

four children were studying there. However, we have been brought here to starve to death as my husband and I have no work. Even today my man has to take the rickshaw several kilometres back to Mall Road in order to fill our stomachs. But it is not feasible for him to cover such a long distance everyday. How will a man work if he repeatedly tires himself in this useless exercise? Thus my husband has no option but to remain in this area. But over here, there is no place where he can stay or keep his rickshaw. Due to lack of proper food and rest my husband has fallen sick. Despite having our own rickshaw we are unable to make the two ends meet. The only alternative left for us is to leave this place and go away.'

This woman also says, 'When we are not in a position to feed ourselves how can we pay the government Rs. 7000 for this plot? And people feel that the poor do not want to live even if they are provided with a place. Hadn't we come to Delhi to earn our daily bread? Compared to this hand-span of a land we have much more land in our native village. If we could leave our own homes in the hope of earning a better living elsewhere, I see no reason why we should have any affection for this worthless place.'

Smita Snehi, an active worker of Jan Parivahan Panchayat went through a similar experience when she met 40 year old Muhammad Rabban, an illiterate man from Mahipabynagama village in Begusarai district of Bihar. Circumstances had compelled him to come all the way to Delhi to drive a rickshaw. Rabban's heart-rending story, narrated below in his own words, is an apt statement of the marginalisation of the urban poor and his further deterioration under globalisation.

> *My name is Muhammad Rabban. I have six children—4 boys and 2 girls out of whom one is married. Except for a house, I have nothing else in the village where I used to work as a craftsman.*
>
> *Not much could be earned in the village as there was little work. It was difficult to make ends meet. My father expired a long time back but my mother is still alive. Since I am the only son, my mother would not permit me to leave*

the village. But sheer helplessness forced me to come here and earn my bread. I have been in Delhi for the last 25 years. I used to live here by myself but 2-3 months back my son (aged 15-16 years) joined me. I am getting him trained in a motor-starter factory so that later in life he can be on his own.

I reside in House no. 2231, Street no. 17, Shanti Nagar, Trinagar. I share a room with 6-7 people of my own village and each of us contributes Rs. 210 for that room since its rent is Rs. 1500. When I came to Delhi I initially worked as a craftsman as it was a profession I was good at. But it involved a lot of hard work and there wasn't much money in it. Moreover, I had to work under someone and I detested it. Gradually I lost interest and left this work after 2-3 years. Some of my fellow-villagers who pulled rick-shaws persuaded me to join them and I too began to drive a rickshaw.

I purchased a rickshaw on instalments and deposited Rs. 500 in the beginning. Then every subsequent month I paid an instalment of Rs. 500. After having paid Rs. 2600I owned a rickshaw. I have been driving it for the last 22 years. My rickshaw is approved by the Delhi Municipal Corporation. I have the license of a rickshaw-owner as well as that of a rickshaw-driver. However, I spent Rs. 60 in get-ting the rickshaw passed. Every year I have to spend money on getting the license renewed since the Delhi Municipal Corporation demands a lot of bribe for passing the rickshaw and renewing the license. To add to my woes, there is scarcity of water in my locality. I get water from a nearby polythene factory. I do not have a ration card as yet though I have made several rounds to the ration office. They, too, ask for a bribe of Rs. 700-800. From where will I manage so much of money? The only time I can afford the luxury of consulting a private doctor is when I'm terribly ill. We cook our food on a stove.

I earn around Rs. 80-100 daily out of which Rs. 40-50 get spent. I manage to save Rs. 50-60 and this saving enables me to visit my village twice or thrice a year. Since the onus lies on me, it is pertinent for me to go there whenever possible but I also ensure that every month Rs. 1000-1500 reach my people so that they are not too tight for two square meals.

I couldn't have any of my kids educated. I feel bad about it. But what could I do? Where from could I have arranged the fees and other expenses? Somehow I was able to bring up my children. A poor man can only think about providing for their meals and not about their education.

Traffic police harasses us. They don't allow us to park the rickshaw anywhere, beat us with their sticks, keep ordering us to remove rickshaws from here and from there. There is no provison of a stand for us. We are not allowed to pick passengers from bus stand or anywhere. They scare us away by their batons. Sometimes they puncture the tyres. When we try to stop them they treat us with the choicest of abuses. Now a days every road is a no-entry area for rickshaws. One never know why when cars can be driven on them, why not rickshaws? There are 50-60 of us who park our rickshaws on the crossing of Trinagar. A leader of this area helps us quite a lot. We couldn't have parked our rickshaws here without his help, otherwise rickshaw theft is a regular feature here.

MCD people are equally ruthless towards us. They seize our rickshaws without a valid reason and without bothering to find

out whether the rickshaw is passed or not. The day they get hold of rickshaw, a fine of Rs. 300 is slapped on us along with a store charge of Rs. 25 daily. It's certainly not easy for a poor man to arrange so much money in no time but we are helpless. If within 15 days we are unable to get our rickshaw released then they even break it.

During the time we visit our native village, no one else is allowed to drive our rickshaw. After all, what's wrong if someone else drives it for a few days to fill his belly? What kind of rules and regulations are these? People from the committee break our rickshaws for no rhyme or reason. All the laws are unfavourable for us.

Still I am content driving the rickshaw though I desperately need more money for my family.

The Altered Relations Between Labour, Employment and Economy

Several rickshaw-drivers like Muhammad Rabban must have come to Delhi in the take 1970s. Compared to those years, the circumstances have altered drastically today. There has been a marked change in the equation between labour, employment and the economy and globalisation has further weakened the strength of the urban poor.

This process has decreased the number of labourers in organised areas and increased their count in unorganised localities. The government only focuses on labourers in the organised areas whenever it plans to provide facilities to workers. Unfortunately, it has no concrete programmes for the development of the workers in the unorganised areas and rickshaw-drivers certainly belong to the latter category.

On the other hand, trade unions have also become feeble. It is easier to unite labourers in organised areas as they work in a certain factory or office where they get an opportunity to meet on a regular basis and discuss their problems. But, in the unorganised sector not only does their work place change, but their jobs also don't remain the same. Once some labourers gain efficiency in a particular jobs, they start taking interest in it. But when it is no longer available to them they are not averse to switching on to other jobs. They are motivated to do so by the pressure to earn their living come what may. We discovered that a lot of craftsmen, working on daily wages in areas surrounding Delhi such as Gurgaon, Faridabad and Loni, drive rickshaws when they do not find any other work. On the other hand, in dire circumstances, several rickshaw-drivers do sundry jobs like working as labourers, whitewashing houses, carrying gas-bulbs during marriages, sweeping and cleaning.

In such a situation no labourer of an unorganised area is willing to regularly participate in the activities of an organisation. A large section of the urban poor is either illiterate or average-literate. Therefore, he is unable to grasp the reasons responsible for his sufferings. But he does realise that he is being manipulated and cheated. Therefore he views government policies issued in his name with a suspicious eye. Even Prime Minister Atal Behari Vajpayee knows that the urban poor is not enthused about globalisation. In a letter to Delhi's Lt. Governor, he wrote, 'The time has come for us to improve the license-system so that the

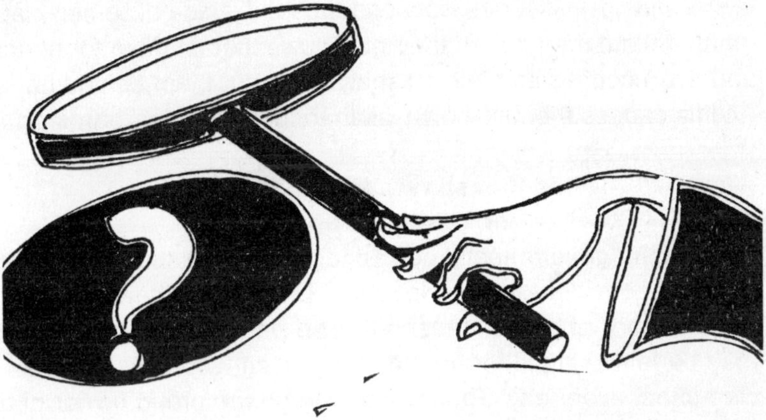

people belonging to lower sections of society like rickshaw-drivers and peddlers can earn their bread without any fear. This change will rightfully convey that policy-reforms are meant to benefit not only the affluent and the middle class but also the poor.'

It is true that the government says one thing and practises another. Since the time the Prime Minister wrote this letter, the police have increased their atrocities on rickshaw-drivers. Most roads display a 'no-entry' sign for rickshaw-wallahs thereby restricting their movement to limited areas. Due to this reason they get fewer passengers as no passenger wants to change rickshaws one after another and make travelling expensive. For instance, a person making to travel from the Yamuna Pushta to Daryaganj will have to take a rickshaw twice as rickshaws are prohibited from evening the Ring Road. However, the temptation to catch a passenger compels rickshaw-drivers to break the

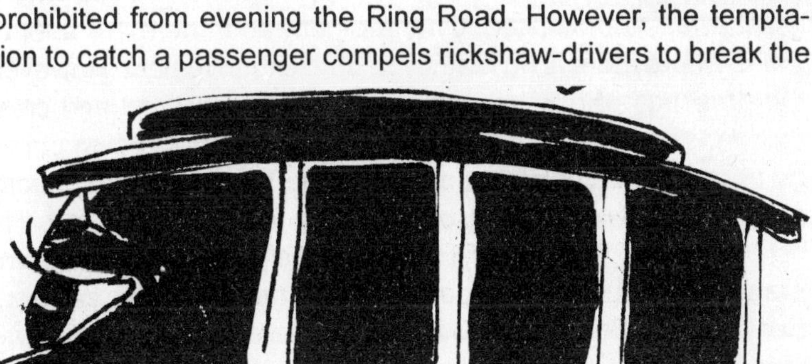

law resulting in serious consequences. Traffic-policemen nab them, deflate the tyres of their rickshaws, detain them for hours and even confiscate their rickshaws and put them behind bars. All this causes the rickshaw-wallah to lose his day's earnings.

Is Rickshaw a Public Means of Transport or Not?

What is the government's perception of the rickshaw and what should it consider this vehicle to be? Does a rickshaw fall under the category of public transport? The answer to this question may be fairly simple for an ordinary citizen who uses this vehicle almost every day. Though he may be the proud owner of a scooter or a car yet his daily life is impossible without a rickshaw. But if the answer to the same query is sought from a legal viewpoint then a completely different picture emerges. According to Delhi's Deputy Commissioner of Traffic Police, Sanjay Beniwal, 'Under the Motor Vehicle Act, there is no specific definition of a rickshaw. Since it comes under the category of slow moving traffic, the provisions made for it are similar to the ones made for cycles and carts. Also, under the Motor Vehicle Act, no other vehicle can be included except motor vehicles. In such a condition, a rickshaw cannot be considered a part of public transport system.'

Beniwal thinks that society's dependence on rickshaws is a result of its helplessness and the day a comprehensive public transport system is established, people will stop using rickshaws. He also says, 'There are some places in Delhi where rickshaws are prohibited. On the other hand, there are a lot of areas where there is no restriction on their movement. However, the presence of rickshaws is an extremely inhuman and cruel fact. In today's modern world the sight of one man being pulled by another is completely unacceptable. The lack of a comfortable and trustworthy transport system forces people to sit in rickshaws and that is why it is imperative for us to have a comprehensive public transportation scheme at the earliest.' Beniwal considers rickshaws a great problem for the traffic system. He feels, 'The biggest problem is the vast number of rickshaws. Officially, the number of licensed rickshaws is only 73,000 whereas at least 5 lakh rickshaws move around on the roads of Delhi. This figure is astounding in itself. Naturally, such a huge number of rickshaws also require lots of space where they can be driven or parked. In such a situation it becomes difficult to control them. Moreover, slow-moving vehicles such as rickshaws cause a lot of accidents. Innumerable accidents used to take place right in front of Jama Masjid but the number considerably decreased once rickshaws were banned in that area. Actually rickshaws move around everywhere but most of Delhi's roads have been constructed keeping in mind a particular kind of traffic. Therefore, the presence of slow-moving traffic affects the entire functioning of general traffic.'

Beniwal believes that if any rickshaw-driver enters a prohibited zone then he should be dealt with strictly. In Beniwal's opinion, legally and

technically a rickshaw-wallah cannot enter a prohibited area. And if he does so, then his rickshaw must be confiscated and handed over to the MCD who break and destroy such rickshaws. Beniwal points out, 'We confiscate rickshaws in two situations. If a rickshaw is caught under the Delhi Police Act then it is returned to the owner provided he shows documental evidence of being the true owner of that vehicle. But if a rickshaw is confiscated under MCD laws, then we hand it over to MCD officials. ... Earlier traffic police used to challan even the pedestrians. When a lot of hue and cry was raised over it, the court had to intervene and protect these poor people. ... Our entire concentration is on regulating the traffic and whoever tries to obstruct its simple functioning will not be spared be it a rickshaw-driver or some one else. ... We cannot permit them to drive on the Ring Road because compared to the Ring Road traffic, their speed is really slow and this increases the possibility of accidents there. Thus if they are found moving in that area they are forcibly removed. ... The complaints (of police taking bribe) are untrue. Protests of rude behaviour are acceptable but it would be wrong to say that police officers demand money. However, corruption has spread to the top-most rungs of the political circle and it will be difficult to eradicate it from its roots. The only recourse is that people become conscientious themselves. ... The argument that rickshaws should be banned doesn't carry much weight but we still have to keep the overall scenario of traffic in mind. After all, the roads are not increasing and we have to make the best use of the available space. Concise and complete provisions should be made regarding the entry of rickshaws in various areas. In the last few years there has been a heavy increase in vehicles per kilometre. Therefore, control must be exercised over the number of rickshaws and certain restrictions must be imposed on them. Who knows in near future a situation may arise wherein to promote a pollution free environment an act allowing only rickshaws and cycles to ply may be passed. Under those circumstances, no one would be able to deny the importance of rickshaws. As of now we need a better transport system.'

Contrary to Beniwal's police-cum-legal viewpoint if things are viewed from an ordinary citizen's perspective it becomes clear that it is the rickshaw-drivers troubling the traffic police but vice-versa. Due to one reason or another routes are changed every other day on Delhi's roads and 'no-entry' signs appear at new places. Unaware of these new developments, ignorant rickshaw-wallah end up violating traffic rules. The end result is that the tyres of their rickshaws are deflated, valves are removed and the driver is beaten-up. Later on he is dragged along with his rickshaw to the police station. Now-a-days even the home-guard makes money from poor rickshaw-owners.

The other problem is that of MCD due to which labourers driving hired rickshaws are always at the receiving end. Whenever a rickshaw is confiscated by a MCD official, its seat is left with the driver so that later he can identify the rickshaw with its help. A rickshaw-driver has to bribe the concerned official(s) so that he can rescue his vehicle otherwise the process is unnecessarily delayed. MCD people are also reluctant to issue driving licenses though this needs to be done only once a year. It's only once in a while that MCD provides adequate space to rickshaw-drivers to park their vehicles. A rickshaw-wallah's life could be easier if the MCD provided him with a parking area equipped with drinking water and toilet facilities. Most of the rickshaw-owners lose their night's sleep worrying about their rickshaws getting stolen. This obviously affects their health. After analysing the relationship between the traffic and all non-motorised vehicles including rickshaws, Dr. Gitam Tiwari concludes in the same vein :

> *Urban transport in Indian cities is heterogeneous. It is dominated by walk trips, non-motorised modes such as bicycles and rickshaws, and motorised para transit and public transport, depending on the size of the city. A high share of non-motorised vehicles (NMVs) and motorised two wheelers (MTW) characterises the transport system of Indian cities.*
>
> *Public transport plays a limited role in cities with population up to 15-20 lakhs. Intermediate public transport (IPT) or para transit modes, both motorised three wheeled tempos and non-motorised cycle rickshaws, play an important role in intra-city travel. However, absolute number of bicycles have been increasing in even mega cities like Delhi. Delhi has an estimated 1.5 million bicycles and 110,000–300,000 cycle rickshaws. In addition to bicycles, non-motorised rickshaws are used for devliery of goods like furniture, refrigerators and washing machines etc. Semi-skilled workers, carpenters, masons, plumbers, postmen,*

and courier services use bicycles. Therefore, the demand for bicycles and rickshaws is in large number at present and is likely to exist in the future also. This situation is not explicitly recognised in policy documents and very little attention is given to improving the facilities for non-motorised modes.

Rickshaws are often viewed as a cause for congestion and as vehicles which violate traffic regulations and cause chaos on the road. However, rickshaws and other non-motorised vehicles in Delhi as well as in other cities have been completely ignored in traffic planning and road designs. The road network is used by at least seven categories of motorised and non-motorised vehicles. Vehicles ranging in width from .60 m to 2.6 m, and capable of maximum speeds ranging from 15 km/h to 100 km/h, share the same road space and carriageway. Traffic is characterised by lack of any effective channelisation, mode segregation or control of speeds.

In the mind of the formally trained planner it looks like chaos moving toward total deadlock. Motor vehicles (MVs) and non-motorised vehicles (NMVs) have different densities at peak traffic hours at different locations of cities. The existing traffic characteristics, modal mix, location details, geometric design, land use characteristics and other operating characteristics present a unique situation where economic and travel compulsions have overwhelmed official plans. On the two and three lane roads, bicycles and other NMVs primarily use the outermost lane on the left, i.e., curb side lane and MVs do not use the left most lanes even at low rickshaw and bicycle densities. Rickshaws and cyclists use the right. Even at one-lane sites rickshaws and cyclists occupy the left extreme giving space to motorised vehicular traffic.

Since primarily bicycles and other non-motorised vehicles use the left side of the road, buses are unable to use designated bus lanes and are forced to stop in the middle lane at bus stops. This disrupts the smooth flow of traffic in all lanes and makes cycling, use of rickshaws and other non-motorised modes more hazardous. Providing a separate bicycle and rickshaw track would make more space available for motorised modes and cycling less hazardous. Clearly, it is the lack of facilities for rickshaws and bicycles and other non-motorised modes which results in congestion and chaos and not the presence of these vehicles in themselves.

Ownership: Legal versus Illegal

Issues related to ownership and its legitimacy have been looked into deeply by Sindhu Menan, who has closely seen the lives and struggles of the urban labour class:

Cycle rickshaws are the only means of transport for most of the residents of say Old Delhi, Ajmeri Gate, Delhi Cantonment area etc. Most of the residential colonies in Old Delhi, Nayi Sarak, Trilokpuri and numerous such colonies have narrow roads where motorised public transport cannot reach. Very few rickshaw-drivers are owners of their rickshaws. Mostly businessmen rent it out. 'We provide these poor folk with employment,' says Raju (name changed) who owns 150 rickshaws. For the last 24 years Raju has been in this business. According to the bye-laws of MCD, licences are issued to five categories of people: owner-driver, joint owner-cum-driver, widows, physically handicapped and driver-not-an-owner. In these categories widows can own five rickshaws. No one else can possess more than one rickshaw. In Delhi there are numerous rickshaw-owners like Raju. A driver owning a rickshaw is a very rare phenomenon.

Same is the case of Arvind (name changed) who owns 500 rickshaws. Arvind is from the Madhubani district of Bihar. He started buying rickshaws in 1994. 'For buying a rickshaw one needs Rs. 3500 minimum, apart from the license fee and other charges etc. How can a migrant labour, who left the village because he couldn't afford even one square meal spend such a huge amount to buy a rickshaw?' Arvind asks. Arvind admits that the business he runs is illegal. 'According to bye-laws of

We cannot Argue that Rickshaws should be Banned

C. P. Gupta
Additional Commissioner,
Municipal Corporation of Delhi

Q. According to MCD how many rickshaw-drivers are there in Delhi?

A. According to the bye-laws of MCD there is no limit in issuing licenses to the rickshaw-drivers. We have fixed 99,000 as the number to issue licences. But till now only 73,000 rickshaws have been given licenses.

People are not coming to take licences. We advertise in the newspapers but even after our continuous effort rickshaw-drivers do not turn up to take licences.

Where the means of transport is not frequently available, cycle-rickshaws are more common. Rickshaw-drivers are seen mostly in the Walled City, Civil Line, Karol Bagh and for trans-Yamuna areas.

Q. According to the law, what is the procedures to issuing a license for a rickshaw?

A. There are twelve zones in Delhi, out of that licences are issued from 11 zones (Narela area, is excluded). We issue notification in the press. Application forms have to be filled up and submitted by the rickshaw-driver. They are called for testing where the height and width of the rickshaw is checked and then the license is issued. The license fee is Rs. 50. We also give them embossed number plates. Till now MCD has issued 73,000 licences. We can issue up to 99,000.

Q. Does MCD consider a rickshaw a public mode of transport?

A. When we are issuing licences it means that we consider it as a valid mode of transport.

Q. What is the criteria required for an individual to own a rickshaw?

A. Any physically fit person can own a rickshaw. What

he will have to do is to fill in the application form, pay Rs. 50 for the rickshaw and Rs. 25 as license fee.

Q. What are the formalities for issuing a driving license for a rickshaw-driver?

A. There are 5 categories of people who are entitled for rickshaws:

(a) Owner rickshaw-driver
(b) Joint owner cum rickshaw-driver
(c) Widows
(d) Handicapped
(e) Rickshaw-driver not an owner.

We advertise usually in the month of November. Licences have to be renewed every year. The renewal fee is the same as the license fee.

Q. How do you decide the no-entry zone? What is the fine or punishment for a rickshaw-driver who enters a no entry zone?

A. No-entry zone is decided according to heavy traffic. NDMC is a no-entry zone and so is the South Zone (Green Park). We never issue license to the South Zone.

Q. What are the procedures that you have to follow to seize a rickshaw? How can a rickshaw-driver or owner retrieve the rickshaw from the godown?

A. We have a team of rickshaw catchers headed by supervisors (LDC rank). They visit different places in five to six jeeps. Licenses of the rickshaw-drivers will be checked and if they do not have it, rickshaws will be impounded. The rule is that rickshaws without licences should be dismantled and the scrap auctioned.

At the same time if the rickshaw is licensed and the rickshaw-driver doesn't have a license we will charge Rs. 300 as fine and Rs. 25 daily as godown storage charge.

Q. How do you identify a captured rickshaw?

A. A rickshaw could be easily identified with its number plate and receipt of license.

Q. According to the Supreme Court judgement, the term 'rickshaw-owners' doesn't exist. But even then there are innumerable of rickshaw-owners with hundreds of rick-

shaws. How do they get licenses and what is the attitude of the MCD towards the owners?

A. Only widows can own five rickshaws. Otherwise no one can have more than one rickshaw. But law breakers require no license for anything. If it comes to our notice we impound the rickshaw and will dismantle it.

Q. Since there are 11 zones where licences are issued, is it possible for the same individual to take rickshaw licences from different zones?

A. No, it is not possible. Rickshaws are given different colours to identify zones. If we come to know about one person owning many rickshaws strict action will be taken.

Q. What are the formalities for workshops for cycle rickshaws? How do they get license? How do they operate?

A. We do not issue licenses for workshops. They are operated on the land of the owner. If they are operating on the road side, MCD can 'chalan' them or even demolish them.

Q. Do you think that rickshaws should be banned?

A. No. In India we do not have a good transport system. Unless and until we have a better mode of transport we cannot argue that rickshaws should be banned. More than that rickshaws are eco-friendly and cheap. The only thing that we can develop is to have rickshaw lanes so that the traffic is not affected. Rickshaw is a slow moving vehicle and no one can say where he will fetch a passenger so it is difficult to allot parking spaces for them.

Q. There are complaints about MCD officials taking bribe. Do you think it is true? If so what should be done to check it?

A. A rickshaw-driver can never complain like that. First of all he refuses to take a license. So he doesn't have any right to complain about the bribe. What they are trying to do is to pass the buck to someone else's shoulders. But there may be officers who take money. It is difficult to put an end to corruption.

(Labour File, Aug.–Sept. 2000)

MCD, a person is not supposed to own more than a single rickshaw. But I have 500 rickshaws,' he says. 'It is the grief of these poor people that drove me to this illegal business. I wanted to be of some help to these people,' he adds.

The average cost of a cycle rickshaw is Rs. 3500. For getting a license officially one has to pay Rs. 50 and unofficially this amount is Rs. 200 to Rs. 250. 'Then come all the expenses of repairing the vehicle, taking it out from the clutches of traffic policemen as well as MCD authorities—all these expenses are met by us,' says Raju.

Article 3(1) of the Cycle Rickshaw Bye-laws of 1960 framed under Section 481 of the Delhi Municipal Corporation Act 1957 says that: 'No persons shall keep or ply or hire a cycle-rickshaw in Delhi unless he himself is the owner thereof and holds a license granted in that behalf by the Commissioner on payment of the fee that may from time to time, be fixed under sub-section (2) of Section 430. It provides that no person will be granted more than one such license; and no person shall drive a cycle rickshaw for hire unless he holds a driving license granted in that behalf by the commissioner on payment of the fee that may, from time to time be fixed under sub-section (2) of Section 430.' There was an amendment in the bye-laws in 1960 that provides further that the Commissioner may grant more than one licence to a widow or a handicapped person subject to the maximum of five licences. It also inserted a new provision 3(2) in the bye-law which says that the licences granted to drivers shall be valid only for a period of three years.

MCD authorities argue that the amendments were done to eliminate the exploitation of rickshaw-drivers by the owners of cycle rickshaws. Under this bye-law only the owner of the cycle rickshaw can obtain a license to keep a cycle rickshaw or to ply for hire and only one such license would be issued to a person. They believe that they comply totally to the bye-laws. 'According to our knowledge individuals own only a single rickshaw. But if there are people who own multiple rickshaws it is totally illegal,' says an MCD officer.

'We had nothing when we came to Delhi, nor are we edu-

cated enough to find a good job. No one was there to help us other than the rickshaw-owner. I really do not understand why these helping hands are being termed illegal,' questions Satpal, a rickshaw-driver in the Old Delhi area. Whenever the rickshaw is taken by the police or MCD authorities it is the owner who pays the fine or bribe to retrieve the rickshaw.

Every year in the month of October-November MCD, the license issuing authority calls for licences. Notifications are issued in newspapers inviting application for licences. 'Any individual who is healthy can own a rickshaw if he pays the nomi-

nal license fee of Rs. 50,' says C.P. Gupta, Additional Commissioner (Headquarters) with Delhi Municipal Corporation. But for the driver, getting a license is not an easy task. As far as the MCD authorities are concerned dispensing of a license is a simple procedure. But according to rickshaw-drivers and owners, 'It is the most difficult task if you are not willing to pay a bribe'.

According to the bye-law: 'Any license to be granted to any person under these bye-laws shall be a license with photograph affixed thereon and expenses incurred thereon shall be borne by the licensee. These charges shall be on actual cost basis as determined by the Commissioner from time to time'. 'In reality, they are very hesitant to issue driving license. If MCD issues a license it will be after taking Rs. 100 to Rs. 150, over and above the actual fee of Rs. 25,' complains a rickshaw-driver. Consequently, in Delhi, very few rickshaw-drivers have licences.

Delhi is divided into zones and licences are issued in these zones. When a rickshaw-driver applies for a license after paying Rs. 50 he will be given an embossed number plate for the rickshaw. Rickshaws under each zone are identified with a particular colour (the

colour varies from zone to zone).

Whenever MCD authorities impound rickshaw they take it to a godown and charge Rs. 300 as fine and Rs. 25 per day as godown charges. 'If you pay money to MCD authorities it is very easy to bring back the rickshaw otherwise they keep on giving excuses,' says Raju.

MCD authorities are not aware of the number of rickshaw-drivers in Delhi. 'We have not undertaken any survey of the rickshaw-drivers in Delhi,' says C. P. Gupta, who is in charge of rickshaw-drivers in Delhi. 'Till now we have issued 73,000 licences and we can issue 26,000 more. But the unofficial estimate of rickshaw-drivers in Delhi will be 5 lakhs', he adds. What it effectively means is that about 4,22,000 odd rickshaw-drivers in the city are illegal and that too with the knowledge of the authorities. In Delhi there are very few rickshaw-drivers who carry valid licences.

When MCD authorities impound a rickshaw it should be relieved in 15 days time. The authorities do not keep the rickshaw after 15 days. They dismantle it and auction the scrap. 'Any cycle rickshaw found plying for hire without a license or found driven by a person not having proper license as provided under bye-law 2(1) and (2) shall be liable to be seized by the Commissioner or a person duly authorised by him in this behalf', states a notification of the Delhi Municipal Corporation (rickshaw bye-laws, 1960) issued on 22 June 1994 by the Department of Urban Development.

The notification further states: 'The cycle rickshaw, so seized shall be disposed off by public auction after dismantling, deformation of such process including smashing it into a scrap after a reasonable time as may be decided by the Commissioner from time to time. The sale proceeds of the public auction after deducting the expenses of the auction and other departmental charges/dues shall be distributed equally amongst owners of the seized cycle rickshaws put to auction, who come forward within 30 days of public auction. In case no owner comes forward for claiming amount then the sale proceeds of public auction shall be deemed to be the municipal funds and the same shall be deposited in the municipal treasury.'

Rickshaw-drivers feel concerned that the amount that has to be paid to relieve an impounded rickshaw is huge. Individuals owning single rickshaws are the ones who are the worst affected. 'In many a case authorities impound the rickshaws on Friday,' says Heerachand who plies his rickshaw in the Mayur Vihar-Trilokpuri area. This means that on Monday if we go to retrieve it, we will have to pay Rs. 300 as fine plus Rs. 100 (Rs. 25 per day, this includes the days of impounding and relieving), he complains. MCD also seizes rickshaws under the MCD Act 66. A majority of the rickshaw-drivers are not aware of any laws. 'I never knew why I was beaten and my rickshaw taken away,' says Laluram who is totally ignorant about rules and regulations.

For traffic policemen rickshaws are the biggest nuisance

element on the road. Since rickshaws come under slow moving traffic, the Motor Vehicles Act is not applicable to them. 'Roads are designed in such a manner that there is no space left for rickshaws,' says Sanjay Beniwal, DCP, Traffic. 'We are concerned about the smooth moving of traffic without any hindrance to the public,' he adds. 'Police beat us brutally', complains a rickshaw-driver in Old Delhi. The only option left for us is to flee when we see a policeman around,' he adds.

Many a time the police impounds a rickshaw as 'lawaris' (illegal). The driver, scared of being beaten up by an approaching policeman leaves the rickshaw and runs away. The responsibility of releasing the rickshaw from the police is that of the owner. 'It is better to pay the police-wallah money, otherwise he will hand it over to the MCD where it is very tedious and expensive to get the rickshaw back,' says Nassimuddin (name

changed). The legal procedure is time consuming. One will have to give an application to the SP which will be forwarded to the Traffic Inspector, who forwards it back to the SP. After verification and SP's signature it is sent back once again to the Traffic Inspector.

Traffic inspector Ravinder Soni says, 'Police may behave roughly with the drivers if they create obstruction to traffic, but taking bribe is out of question. Who will dare to take money from these poor folks who work desperately to make both ends meet,' he says.

'My rickshaws never face problems from the police or committee people,' says Arvind. 'Every month I meet them personally and pay so that my rickshaws are free from their clutches.' 'We are not cheating any one. We sweat and earn our daily bread. Why are we ill-treated like this?' asks Manoj who is a driver in the Delhi South Zone. 'Even the passengers do not have any sympathy for us. They argue even for 50 paise. We are always at the receiving end,' says another rickshaw-driver

The experience of rickshaw-owners and drivers regarding the attitude of the administration varies. The investigation of Jan Parivahan Panchayat also proves this point. Do officials authorised to pass rickshaws have the required technical knowledge? According to 26.6 per cent rickshaw-owners, they don't, 71.4 per cent owners answer in the affirmative. Should there be a separate lane on roads for rickshaw and cart-drivers? A majority 91.4 per cent rickshaw-owners feel yes whereas the rest disagree. Now and then the Delhi Municipal Corporation confiscates rickshaws and breaks them if they are not claimed back in time. In this context, 74.3 per cent owners condemn the practice while 5.7 per cent feel that these rickshaws should be auctioned and 20 per cent opine that the 'challan' fee in such cases should be decreased. In fact, rickshaw-owners have several complaints against the Delhi Municipal Corporation. 25.7 per cent feel that the rules laid down for passing a rickshaw are flawed, 2.9 per cent owners complain that the corporation does not apprise them of traffic rules and the same percent all of rickshaw-owners has a grudge against the corporation for not giving licenses the whole year round, 2.9 per cent owners hold the corporation responsible for not providing them facilities like parking stands, toilets and night-shelters. Another 2.9 per cent owners protest against the ban on rickshaws in different areas; 17.1 per cent rickshaw-owners raise their voice against the exorbitant passing fees whereas 31.4 per cent of them express disillusionment over other issues. However, there are 14.3 per cent rickshaw-owners who have no complaints against the corporation.

Delhi's rickshaw-owners are also dissatisfied with the traffic police. While 11.4 per cent owners find the no-entry provision justifiable, 2.9 per cent are angry at not finding the no-entry board anywhere. As far as the matter of tyres being deflated and rickshaw-drivers being beaten-up are concerned, 17.1 per cent owners complain against each and 11.4 per cent strongly oppose the handing over of confiscated rickshaws by traffic police to Delhi Municipal Corporation in the same time. 2.9 per cent rickshaw-owners register some other kinds of complaints and 37.1 per cent of them have no problem with the traffic police. When the rickshaws are 'challaned', 85.7 per cent owners give bribe to get them released and 8.6 per cent resort to pleading.

The percentage of lucky rickshaw-owners whose vehicles have never been caught rests at 5.7. On the question of whether rickshaws benefit our society, the owners express diverse viewpoints: 8.6 per cent consider rickshaws an excellent vehicle for short distances, 31.4 per cent say that they ply on all roads and even drop you home, 5.7 per cent regard rickshaws cheap and easily available for commuting, 22.9 per cent owners perceive them to be a good means of earning a livelihood, 25.7

per cent feel they are pollution-free vehicles and 5.7 per cent view them as a comfortable mode of transport.

Identity Crisis: For Want of Struggle and Organisation

No community is devoid of problems. Difficulties that persist at a personal level can be sorted out individually but those that exist at a macro level can only be encountered with a collective and unified effort. While some issues get solved by discussions at the political level, others require agitations and campaigns as solutions. And it is here that the need for an organisation is felt. Rickshaw-drivers, rickshaw-owners and rickshaw-mechanics—all feel that they lack a union and this point is further proven by the facts and figures that have come to the fore in the survey conducted by Jan Parivahan Panchayat.

Be it any Indian citizen, it has become an absolute must for him to have a ration-card and an election I-card. He requires these in various situations—to get a passport made or to get immediate reservation in a train. Similarly, to purchase sugar or kerosine oil from a government fair-price shop (ration shop) he needs a ration-card. Most of the rickshaw-drivers are from areas outside Delhi and therefore they face a lot of problem in acquiring both these documents. Officials from the ration-office prevaricate when it comes to making ration-cards for the poor. They usually demand Rs. 200-400 as bribe to do the needful. Since most of the rickshaw-drivers are either illiterate or semi-literate they are scared to go near the ration-office and demand that their work be done. Similarly, getting the election I-card made is an equally tough task for the process involves submitting a copy of a person's ration-card (having names of all the family members) in the office. The result is that in the region 73.3 per cent (87.4 per cent in Delhi) drivers do not have ration-cards. As a natural consequence, in this region 73 per cent (90.7 per cent in Delhi) names of rickshaw-drivers do not figure in voting lists since they don't have election I-cards, hence they are unable to participate in the election-process. It means that these rickshaw-wallahs are being deprived of the status of being ordinary citizens of India. The case of rickshaw-drivers in Rajasthan is different since their local status enables them to put some pressure on the concerned officials through their representatives. Their condition is certainly better—66.7 per cent have ration-cards, 60.9 per cent have election I-cards, 71.3 per cent have their names in voting-lists and can exercise all their voting rights.

Around 92 per cent rickshaw-drivers have no information about the existence of a union in their respective cities. The main reason behind this is that these people are not alert enough about their rights and ignorantly bear afflictions accepting them as their destiny. Moreover, in these cities there is a scarcity of strong rickshaw unions that can be in constant contact with rickshaw-wallahs. Very few rickshaw-drivers know how much money needs to be spent in getting a rickshaw passed. More the people, more the speculation. Someone says Rs. 10, someone else quotes Rs. 150-200. 69 per cent rickshaw-drivers in Haryana and 34 per cent in Uttar Pradesh are not in a posi-

tion to say anything about the license fees. The reason behind this is that usually it is the rickshaw-owners who get the licenses made on their own. When a rickshaw-driver applies for a license, he never gets a fair deal. They are usually illiterate or very little read. These poor people do not even get the receipt read from someone after the license has been issued to them but the process they undergo to get the license does make them realise that something is definitely wrong with the system. In other cities where the license fee is comparatively less and where drivers have to face less arbitrariness, they offer a more lucid explanation of the process: 22 per cent drivers in Haryana and 32.6 per cent in Uttar Pradesh state that the license fee being charged is fair though 9 per cent and 33.4 per cent respectively rate it as extremely high.

Rickshaw-drivers are also not fully aware of the challan tariffs: 66 per cent drivers in Haryana and 55 per cent in Uttar Pradesh are ignorant about it. However, 32 per cent and 26 per cent respectively have nothing to say against 'challans'. In Uttar Pradesh, 12 per cent drivers say that the 'challan fee' is not fixed. Struggling with problems like challan, license and police atrocities, rickshaw-drivers feel the need for an organisation. About 99 per cent say that there must be a rickshaw union. City authorities in places like Delhi destroy the confiscated rickshaws and hence 67.2 per cent drivers feel that this practice should be stopped. 16.7 per cent say that the caught rickshaws should be released on payment of fines and 3.8 per cent opine that the rickshaw union should protest against such issues.

Time and again, police and traffic police keeps taking action against rickshaws. Do they confiscate rickshaws or 'challan' them? 91.9 per cent drivers answer this question in the negative. But 3.1 per cent drivers in Haryana and 57.1 per cent in Delhi say yes, 95.5 per cent drivers feel that they have not been bothered by police or traffic police as far as confiscating rickshaws or imposing fines is concerned. Merely 4.5 per cent say yes. In Haryana, Uttar Pradesh and Delhi—2.3 per cent, 0.8 per cent and 28.6 per cent respectively answer in the affirmative. Rickshaw-owners have to adopt different strategies to get their confiscated rickshaws released. 50 per cent (60 per cent in Delhi) owners say that they have to take recourse to bribe. 21.4 per cent feel that paying 'challan' fee helps and 28.6 per cent vote in favour of trying some other means.

Compared to rickshaw-drivers, rickshaw-owners are more aware. About 59 per cent have no information about a rickshaw union in their area though 41 per cent of them do. In this context, this percentage is about four times that of rickshaw-drivers. It is due to this awareness that in several cities there are unions of rickshaw-owners no matter how slack they might be. From time to time, these unions hold 'dharnas' and demonstrations on problems associated with rickshaws. But according to survey figures only 19.2 per cent of the rickshaw-owners participate in such protest demonstrations whereas the rest don't.

Rickshaw-mechanics too are harassed by the police. Several mechanics who fix a particular place to sit and work are pestered to remove their seat or else pay illegal money. In the Delhi zone, 12.3 per cent rickshaw-artisans complain that the police constantly intervenes and compels them to change their place of work. But 87.7 per cent craftsmen also say that they have faced no police-pressure at all. Apart from the police, city authorities also carry out campaigns to remove rickshaw-mechanics' road-side seats by taking help, at times, of hooligans and rogues. Moreover, garage-owners do not pay these people sufficient salaries. All these problems perplex rickshaw-mechanics who are unable to demand their rights collectively as they are spread out in the city. During conversations, they too express the need for a union but things can only change if someone takes an initiative to lead.

In Delhi, there are unions of rickshaw-drivers and owners. However, there is no organisation of this kind for rickshaw-mechanics, producers or passengers. Apart from a few unions, the rest are feeble and weak because their meetings and activities are irregular. Moreover, their office-bearers seriously lack synchronisation. Be it a leftist rickshaw-drivers' union or some other rickshaw-drivers' union, the struggle is more with rickshaw-owners than with the government. Ironically, these unions are hardly perturbed by more critical issues like the proposed government policy to exclude rickshaws from the transport system. In such circumstances, there is a dire need for rickshaw-owners, drivers, mechanics and producers to comprehensively unite and build a common platform for struggle because whenever unions have fought collectively they have achieved success. In fact, Delhi's rickshaw-unions provide a perfect example in this case. Similarly the union of rickshaw-owners in Meerut got its demands accepted only due to its united effort. If rickshaw-owners and drivers fight amongst themselves then it will cause serious damage to the rickshaw business.

Rickshaw unions are hardly involved in creative activities. By involving themselves in the training of rickshaw-drivers, they can certainly strengthen the latter's work efficiency and their desire to struggle. For this night-schools can be arranged, every fortnight a meeting can be held and every six months a general meeting can be conducted. Moreover, on special occasions relevant functions can be organised. But all this will be possible only when unions increase their members and inspire them to be active. Union office-bearers can never achieve this if they do not befriend rickshaw-drivers and continue with their officer-like attitude. Unions can also take an initiative to form co-operative-societies for the benefit of the drivers. This will enable them to tackle problems in a systematic manner. Several rickshaw-drivers do not have rickshaws and face other difficulties like lack of proper food and shelter. The societies can provide them rickshaws so that they are not exploited. Also food and night-shelters can be offered to the drivers at cheap rates by these societies. Arrangements too can be made to get their rickshaws repaired. In such a situation, the confrontation between rickshaw-owners and drivers will be impossible. The biggest hurdle in bringing rickshaw-drivers together is their irregularity at work since most of them return to their native villages after a few months. But still drivers can be united if these unions make an earnest attempt. Rickshaw-drivers of Narang Colony, Keshavpuram have proved this point.

Some Positive Modes of Struggle

Delhi, the largest city of the region, has the maximum number of rickshaws and the maximum restrictions on them as well. Also, incidences of struggle happen to be most here to ensure that rickshaws are placed at par with other vehicles on the roads. There are several rickshaw unions in Delhi. Their collective effort has drawn the attention of the Municipal Corporation, State and Central Government and forced them to make certain favourable declarations. Till today, those decisions only exist on paper. The wide-spread corruption in Municipal Corporation is such that its officials ensure that the positive policies made by peoples' representatives are never put to practice. Time and again, rickshaw-unions have approached the court but due to red-tapism even the court orders have been ignored. For instance, the court decision to have boards put for rickshaw-stands at various places was taken in 1982. But still it has not been completely implemented.

However one thing is undeniable—whether rickshaw unions are active or feeble, to a great extent their collective effort has managed to solve problems related to rickshaw-owners and drivers. Moreover, this community has understood that red-tapism will never allow a favourable response and the authorities can be pressurised into reacting positively only through a united struggle.

Jan Parivahan Panchayat talked to several unions operating in Delhi. Chandar Singh Mehrat is the general secretary of the West Delhi Rickshaw-puller's Association. Mehrat is BA pass and has been driving the rickshaw for the last nine years. His rickshaw-drivers' association was established in 1982 and today boasts of 8,200 members. Discussing how this union came into being, Mehrat says, 'A few of us used to drive school-children home. One day fellow-rickshawwallah was slapped by a policeman. Later when he narrated the incident to us we realised that in order to encounter police terror we need an organisation. Thus we consulted B. C. Ganguly, a social worker aware of legal subtleties, and got the organisation registered on 2 January, 1982. That very year around 60-70 rickshaw-drivers became our members.'

This association taught rickshaw-drivers to fight for their problems and the issue of police atrocities was dealt with through collective response. Even now if someone misbehaves with a rickshaw-driver—abuses him or beats him up—other rickshaw-drivers instantly unite and question that person's intentions. This attitude has affected hooligans and police alike who think twice before harassing rickshaw-drivers unnecessarily. According to Mehrat, earlier top police officers used to be concerned about the difficulties faced by rickshaw-wallahs and this improved the behaviour of local policemen towards them. 'Later when the number of members increased', Mehrat says, 'we (the organisation) managed to put pressure on the officers to get our work done. For instance, the people at Nagar Nigam were compelled to make licenses for us. This led more people to join our association since getting a license made is a tough job for any rickshaw-driver. They also realised that to fight corruption and atrocities joining an organization is a must.' Taken aback by the success of the union, rickshaw-contractors and hooligans started attacking rickshaw-drivers whenever they were found alone. Thereafter the members of the union started moving around in groups. To tackle the problem of inebriated rickshaw-drivers, union workers befriended them and discussed their problems. This led to a drastic decrease in their habit of inebriation and several drivers gave up this addiction forever. Illiterate rickshaw-drivers were made to learn counting up to 100 so that in case of an accident they could at least note down the number of the vehicle involved. Literate members of the organisation were encouraged to read aloud from a newspaper to the rest of the members so that they could keep abreast of world news. Attempts were also made to inspire rickshaw-drivers to become more aware. In fact, this endeavour continues to date.

According to Mehrat, their union membership is increasing every day because rickshaw-drivers are realising its usefulness. However, due to certain limitations, the organisation has not been able to increase its activities. First, the association does not have sufficient workers who can expedite its work. Second, the association is careful about not admitting members who might join for vested interests and exploit rickshaw-drivers later. The motive of the organisation is to expand its horizon gradually. Many a times it has failed to convince the authorities about certain issues but whatever the union has achieved is due to its collective struggle.

Pramod Kumar Singh who is the national secretary of the Akhil Bhartiya Cycle-Rickshaw Rozgar Association and the President of its Delhi Branch says, 'Our organisation was established in 1997. Earlier I had been an office-bearer in the Lok Mazdoor Sangh and the Delhi State Cycle-Rickshaw Rozgar Association. Through all these organisations we tried to fight for the welfare of rickshaw-owners and drivers. Our endeavour has always been to unite with other rickshaw unions and struggle collectively for a common cause.'

When did the need to form a union arise? Pramod Kumar answers this question by narrating an experience. 'In 1981 I had five rickshaws, two of them were confiscated by the Municipal Corporation workers. According to them those rickshaws could only be permitted to ply if I paid Rs. 10 every month or if I got their licenses made. This happened on the third day after my rickshaws started moving on the roads. Similarly a few days later, one of my rickshaws was caught in the city zone. Till 1988, I managed to get my rickshaws released from Municipal Corporation only by paying money or through some other means. At that time only 20,000 rickshaws in Delhi were permitted to get their license made. To fight this terror perpetrated by the workers, we formed the Worker's Union and in 1988 we demonstrated against their high handedness in a Municipal Corporation office situated at Bholanath Nagar. The second demonstration was held in 1989 at Raj Niwas. It was only due to these efforts that the Municipal Corporation workers backtracked.'

According to Pramod Kumar, 'There had been a marked decrease in cases of rickshaw-drivers' harassment because of the union's strength. But in 1993 they were in trouble again when there was a big campaign to mass arrest rickshaw-drivers. The various unions in Delhi fought against it jointly. On 1 September, 1993 all rickshaws in Delhi went on a strike and on 2 September, drivers parked rickshaws at Red Fort and demonstrated at Town Hall. This compelled Municipal Corporation officials to negotiate terms with them. Thus, the number of licensed rickshaws to ply in Delhi was raised from 20,000 to 50,000. Rickshaws with 29 inch bodies were also permitted to be driven.'

Delhi Rickshaw Chalak Union is a leftist outfit and Alam Ansari is its president. In Delhi, this union has 40 branches and 17,000 rickshaw-drivers as members. Ansari points out, 'There are around 5 lakh rickshaw-drivers in the city. Naturally, it's a small number of people who are spread out in various parts of the capital. Since economism, casteism and communalism have affected the entire society, rickshaw-wallahs too are its victims and to shake them out of their slumber is a difficult task. But we have an optimistic approach and that is why we are adamantly fighting for the rights of rickshaw-drivers.' Regarding the formation of his union Ansari says, 'I came to Delhi in 1966 and drove rickshaw for a year and a half. In those days rickshaw-drivers faced four kinds of problems—police atrocities, oppression from Municipal Corporation officers, harassment by anti-social elements and trouble from rickshaw contractors. It was to create awareness against these cruelties that in 1974 we formed this union. Since then, this organisation has motivated rickshaw-drivers to struggle against odds. However, the alliance between these four kinds of forces (police, Municipal Corporation, anti-social elements and rickshaw-owners) is such that it cannot be easily broken. Our fight has resulted in some achievements such as the government now allow 99,000 rickshaws in the city (against the previous figure of 20,000). It is a different thing altogether that for a long time the rickshaws plying in the city are about five times what is mentioned in the records.'

The president of Delhi Rickshaw-Chalak-Malik Sangharsh Morcha is Muhammad Islam and the general secretary is Shribhagwan Jaisawal. The organisation circulated this piece of good news through a pamphlet: The fine of Rs. 300 + 25 on licensed rickshaws in Delhi will be abolished; all rights given to traffic police and local police to control rickshaws will be taken back; the drivers will no longer be forced to acquire driver's license and the law approving breaking or auctioning of non-licensed rickshaws will be obliterated. Such rickshaws will now be released after the payment of a fine. Licensed rickshaws will be registered and all unions will be taken into consideration before the formulation of any new policy.

The pamphlet specified that these decisions were taken in a meeting between the president of the standing council of the Municipal Corporation, Rambabu Sharma and a delegation from the 'morcha' in May 2002. Highlighting the need to form this 'morcha', Shribhagwan Jaisawal points out, 'In 1993, the commissioner of Municipal Corporation, Virendra Singh passed an order for confiscation of rickshaws which managed to bridge the gap between rickshaw-owners and drivers who got together to fight this injustice. As I was the secretary of the Delhi Cycle-Rickshaw Mazdoor Union since then my union has been an integral part of this 'morcha' which has worked time and again for the benefit of rickshaw-wallahs. It was at that time that we got the permission to have 50,000 rickshaws licensed instead of 20,000.'

Shribhagwan opts in favour of a policy that keeps a check on the number of rickshaws in the city and yet ensures that rickshaw-drivers are not without work. According to him, 'We must understand the needs of all the people moving on the road. Therefore, rickshaws cannot be allowed to increase at an unstoppable speed. Moreover, rickshaw-drivers must be made to learn the rules of the road so that the chances of accidents can be minimised.' In this context he also points out that, 'We need to improve ourselves. Often drivers do not park rickshaws one after the other. Instead they make a crowd which increases the possibility of traffic jams and irks the public. We must not excuse ourselves by blaming other vehicles of committing the same mistake. Actually rickshaw-wallahs desperately need training which the unions are unable to provide due to lack of facilities. Rickshaw-owners are merely concerned about the rent and rickshaw-drivers are only bothered about their earning—this self-centerd attitude is harming the rickshaw business. For any business to do well, it is necessary for people to cooperate and maintain discipline. Similarly, the rickshaw business can only grow if we give it our best. Only then will we make a positive intervention in the traffic policy.'

Rickshaw-owners and drivers in West Delhi have a union called the Cycle-Rickshaw Pullers-Owners' Welfare Association (West Zone). The vice-president of this organisation, Suresh Kakkar opines, 'There have been two obstructions for rickshaw-drivers—Municipal Corporation and traffic police. Right now we are more concerned about traffic police which is prohibiting the entry of rickshaws on more and more roads. At least the Municipal Corporation is only bothered about non-licensed rickshaws now and is not catching the licensed rickshaws anymore. Earlier even the licensed rickshaws were caught on the pretext that drivers did not have driver's license. But no one can match the traffic police in its arbitrariness. It catches rickshaws in the no-entry zone and shows them as abandoned. Everyday as many as 300-400 rickshaws are declared abandoned which is a pack of lies. Now even the rickshaws confiscated and kept in police stations are disappearing which clearly proves that they are being secretly sold.' Suresh Kakkar does not approve of unlicensed rickshaws. He says, 'We want every rickshaw to be licensed and each driver to have legal right to keep a licensed rickshaw. The city should increase the number of licensed rickshaws. Presently the number of licenses can't go beyond the stipulated figure of 99,000. However, a limit on the maximum number of rickshaws to be allowed in the city must be fixed because otherwise there will be an unprecedented rise and this will lead to a situation where drivers already in the rickshaw business will lose their jobs.'

According to a piece of information there are several organisations in Delhi. Although these associations get together to fight for common issues, they lack unity and have not been able to influence the government's policy-making process.

Moreover, two important areas of the city—the New Delhi Municipal Corporation and the Delhi Cantonment Council do not have any kind of rickshaw union.

Haryana's Faridabad district has a rickshaw-drivers' union but it does not have any association of rickshaw-owners or mechanics. The name of the existing union is Rickshaw Chalak Vikas Society and it was registered on 3 December, 2001. The president of this organisation is Prem Mehta, it's general secretary is R. K. Singh and the office of this union is at Nehru Ground. The office-bearers and workers of the organisation can be seen working with great determination. Some of their main activities include getting I-cards made for drivers and solving their daily problems. They have also consistently made efforts to write letters to the Mayor and the Commissioner of the Municipal Corporation apprising them of the problems of rickshaw-wallahs. In a letter to the Mayor, the president of the union requested that, 'the Municipal Corporation may charge road tax from rickshaws and in return give them tokens and provide them with suitable stands.'

In another letter to the Municipal Corporation's senior architect, the general secretary R. K. Singh wrote that, 'The vacant land in front of the Dusshera ground bus stand may be utilised to make a night-shelter for rickshaw-drivers. The hall-like structure may comprise four big rooms with small almirahs where these homeless rickshaw-wallahs may keep their stuff and rest. The union is willing to look after the proposed shelter's maintenance.' Before this union came into being, another rickshaw union called the Faridabad Rickshaw Union was active. However, presently its activities are at a standstill. The president of this erstwhile union is B. K. Pradhan. Even this organisation had requested officials of the Municipal Corporation to provide stands and night shelters to rickshaw-wallahs. Apart from this, it also provided I-cards to drivers and fined those who were found without them. According to one rickshaw-driver, 'This union oppressed rickshaw-drivers instead of benefiting them because every driver was compelled to acquire an I-card. Moreover, members were not admitted in the union voluntarily—rather they were forced to join. At every rickshaw stand, some rickshaw-drivers chosen by the union extracted money for donation and this account was never made transparent to the drivers. Naturally, the union misappropriated the money and distributed it amongst its select members.' Another rickshaw-driver says, The Faridabad union has lost its strength because it neither worked for the welfare of rickshaw-wallahs nor came to their rescue when they needed help. It only organised religious programmes through which it conveniently raised funds for vested interests. It was aided by the police in this venture. Though the Faridabad Rickshaw Union began work in 1978, rickshaw-drivers have got rid of it now. There is another union which has come into existence and it remains to be seen what relation it establishes with rickshaw-wallahs.'

In Panipat, the rickshaw union was formed by Comrade Ramdutta who called it the Cycle-Rickshaw Chalak Union and remained its president from 1966 to 1972. Commenting on how the union was established, Ramdutta points out that, 'In those days rickshaw-drivers were beaten up by the police and the rickshaw-owners demanded more rent from drivers. These helpless victims neither found help from owners nor from the government. They did not even have rickshaw stands. Some rickshaw-drivers arbitrarily took fare from passengers. Keeping all these problems in mind we formed the rickshaw union so that we could bring justice to both the drivers and the passengers.'

Comrade Ramdutta is a freedom fighter. He agrees that despite independence there isn't much change in the lives of the downtrodden. The nature of government policies is such that it provides very little relief to the poor. Comrade Ramdutta says, 'In those days the government had fixed the rate of a tyre at Rs. 9 but shopkeepers were selling it at Rs. 22. Since I repaired cycles and had a repair-shop of my own, I had all the information. Through the union we tried to help rickshaw-wallahs in every way such as getting their rickshaws repaired at cheap rates, buying rickshaw parts for them at lesser price, providing medical assistance to drivers and rescuing them from money lenders. We even arranged an easy bank loan facility for them. Today the rickshaw-drivers in Panipat are in a very bad state because unfortunately, rickshaw-owners inf Panipat have captured their leadership. In fact they exploit them, but on the other hand claim to protect their interests.'

One rickshaw owner points out, 'The rickshaw unions here do not focus on day-to-day problems. Yes, its office-bearers do meet the police or officials of the city council in case any one of us is in trouble. People like us dare not enter a top-notch officer's room on our own so having union people with us does help. The union also assists us in finding stolen rickshaws.'

According to another rickshaw-driver, the rickshaw-owners dominate the unions. Therefore, due attention is certainly paid towards union members, but the owners have no concern for the problems of drivers outside the union.

In Rohtak, there are separate unions of rickshaw-owners and rickshaw-drivers. The owners' union is called the Rohtak Shahar Rickshaw Malik Union and its president is Ram Niwas Verma. One rickshaw-owner feels that, 'The rickshaw-owners' union in Rohtak is not successful. The reason is lack of unity. Every owner follows his own whims and fancies. There is no sense of discipline. This union has been active for the last three months but in previous years each time we formed a union it disintegrated.' According to another owner, 'In order to run the union, it is necessary for every member to pay a membership fee. Earlier the annual membership fee of our union was Rs. 100 and now it is only Rs. 20. But if people show reluctance in paying even Rs. 20, how can the union function?'

There is continuous growth in the number of rickshaws in the city. New owners have joined the rickshaw business and older owners have added more rickshaws to their business. However, the number of drivers in the city has not increased at the same rate. As one rickshaw owner points out, 'No matter how many rickshaws an owner has, some are always standing on the road as no rickshaw-wallah wants to drive an old rickshaw. Moreover, due to lack of coordination between owners, more and more rickshaws are becoming defective. Now the owners have realised their problems and though late in their endeavor, they have at least begun discussions on it. The union took a decision two months ago that in the coming two months no owner will buy a new rickshaw and whoever disobeys, will have to pay Rs. 500 as fine. All the rickshaw-owners have followed this decision.'

Pointing out the difficulties of the owners, the president of the rickshaw-owners' union, Ram Niwas Verma says, 'Since drivers from outside the city do not have I-cards, they run away with rickshaws. The police demands money from the owners if it manages to find the stolen vehicles. It is the owners' helplessness that makes them hand-over rickshaws in unknown hands.' Ram Niwas also says, 'There is a strange misconception in society according to which rickshaw-drivers are perceived to be poor and rickshaw-owners are considered to be rich. Thus, the former are seen as the oppressed and the latter as the oppressors. Once a driver committed suicide by consuming poison. His family members demanded Rs. 15,000 from the rickshaw owner and filed a case against him. They alleged the owner of having harassed the driver to pay the remaining rent for the rickshaw soon—a reason that compelled him to take such a serious step. Had the owner not pressurised the driver so much, accused the family members, he would never have taken this drastic action.' Ram Niwas also says, 'Drivers do not pay the rent on time and when they are constantly pressed by the owners to do so, they start driving some other owner's rickshaw. Obviously, this process makes the first owner's rent unrecoverable forever. There is hardly any owner who does not have a couple of thousands of rupees lying with the driver in this state. Now, all the owners ponder over these problems together and through the union we collectively try to find solutions. Although we lack unanimous opinion on any issue yet we are close to one another. I am sure if we have the same attitude then one day we will emerge stronger as an association.'

In Rohtak there are two drivers' unions. Their main centre of activities is completely different. While one union is active at the Rohtak Bus Terminal, the other operates from the railway station. The former is called Azad Rickshaw Chalak Kalyan

Sangh and its president is Balwant Rai according to whom, 'Our's is a state level union and I am its president since 1977. Through protest, dharnas and letters of representations highlighting the concerns of drivers, we have approached the deputy commissioner of Rohtak and officials of the Municipal Council several times. Our union has demanded that a yellow or pink ration card be made for drivers, easy and cheap house-loan instalments be arranged for them and free health services be provided to their children. Also, stands with shades be made available to rickshaw-drivers. The union has also been solving drivers' personal problems and extending financial aid to them. According to Balwant Rai, all of them pool in their resources whenever any driver's daughter is to be married or someones seriously ill in his family and needs medical help. 'Although the amount collected is quite small yet it shows a bond of mutual love and concern. Once when a driver committed suicide all of us got together and arranged six months ration and clothing for his family.'

One year ago Jan Parivahan Panchayat's team had visited Rohtak and found that every rickshaw-driver who entered the bus depot paid Rs. 2 and got a receipt in return. One rickshaw-driver informed them, 'This receipt is given everyday, that means a driver has to pay Rs. 60 monthly to the Union. It does not benefit an average driver. Only people associated with the union get some advantage out of it. A similar receipt is handed over by the other union operating from the railway station which is a city level organisation and is called Uttar Railway Rickshaw Chalak Association. Its general secretary is Surajbhan and the president is Ranvir Singh Arya. There was an agreement between the two unions that no matter where the receipt is given from, it will be acknowledged by the other union. This means that a driver can pick up a passenger from either the bus depot or the railway station.'

In Rewari, there are separate unions for rickshaw-drivers and owners. Although Rickshaw Chalak Union is in the name of drivers, it addresses problems related to both drivers and owners. This union tries to put pressure on the authority by presenting its demands through 'dharnas' and demonstrations. But the authorities are unsympathetic and they are doing away with whatever little facilities were available earlier. For instance, there used to be a big shaded stand at the railway crossing. A revenue sub-collector bribed a prominent person to get it removed and had a shop built there instead. Drivers have a complaint against owners that they increase the price of rickshaw to Rs. 6500–7000 (whereas it costs only Rs. 3000–3200) before it is offered to them on rent. On the contrary, drivers should be given facilities to repay this amount. Ramswarup, a rickshaw-owner in Rewari says, 'Whenever an owner or a driver is in trouble, I help them by meeting people in authority and influencing them.' But a rickshaw-driver in Rewari feels that no union here is strong enough. The fact remains that no matter how feeble these unions might be, they are benefiting the owners and drivers in some way. 'For example, we are saved from police oppression since we carry union I-cards. If the union had paid more attention to drivers, it would have even succeeded in curbing their bad habits,' says he.

In Rewari, there are personal differences between local drivers and drivers from outside the city. Unfortunately, the union has not been able to play an active role in resolving the matter. Though the union puts these problems across to the authorities yet the lack of any creative programme amongst the drivers renders it incapable of uniting them.

In Uttar Pradesh's Meerut district, there is no drivers' union these days although attempts were made in the past to form a union. The president of the Kalyanam Karoti Sanstha, Kulbhushan Bakshi says, 'In 1950 there were about 4,000 rickshaws and 20 rickshaw stands in this city. At that time I was a third year college student. With the co-operation of some social workers and students, a union was established and called the Rickshaw Karmchari Union. This union provided water facility to drivers at every rickshaw stand. The stands also had air pumps and certain tools for the drivers. In those days the police troubled the rickshaw-wallahs a lot, imprisoned them and filed arbitrary cases against them. Hence, a team of lawyers was arranged by the union that came to the drivers' rescue whenever they were in difficulty and fought their cases for free.'

According to Bakshi, 'The drivers paid one *anna* to the union everyday and this was entered in the card that they were provided by the union. In case of a fine, 50 per cent expense was borne by the union and the rest of 50 per cent was taken care of by the driver himself. The entire expenditure of the case was borne by the union. In several other matters too this union helped the drivers. I worked with it for rwo years and then left it since I had to go to Dehradun for my job.'

According to Bakshi, the rickshaw-driver's rent should be included in the cost of the rickshaw. When the price of the rickshaw becomes equal to its rent, the owner should willingly hand over the ownership to the driver.

The president of the Uttar Pradesh branch of the All India consumer's council, Virendra Gupta says that in 1981 he established an organisation called the Rickshaw Chalak Labour Cell. 'Through this association we tried to work for the benefit of drivers but one office-bearer of our organisation (who was a driver himself) misbehaved with a passenger. Due to this unfortunate incident, our organisation disintegrated in six months and I also parted ways with it.'

The rickshaw-owners' association of this city is called the Merrut Rickshaw-Swami Sangathan. It was established in 1982 but it has been active only for the last three years. The president of this union is Bharat Bhushan Sharma. His rickshaw garage is in Shastri Nagar. According to him, 'There are better relations between owners due to the union's activities and we have even succeeded in pressing the concerned authorities to accept our demands.' Another office-bearer of the organisation, Muhammad Sharif Kureshi says, 'We meet twice a month. Once only the office-bearers meet but the second time all the members of the union get together. In these meetings we discuss rickshaw related problems and think of possible solutions.'

The Lal Jhanda Rickshaw Mazdur Ekta Union in Rajasthan's Alwar district is associated with the working class branch of the Marxist Communist Party. The office of this rickshaw-drivers' union is near Purusharthi Dharamshala and its slogan is—*Rickshaw kiska, chalaye jiska* (Rickshaw belongs to the one who drives it).

The I-cards issued to the drivers by this union mention four instructions—it is the duty of rickshaw-drivers to submit the list of wrong-doers to the union office or police; drivers must park their rickshaws at the allotted stands; in case a passenger forgets his luggage, a driver ought to hand it over to the office or the police and all rickshaw-drivers must abide by traffic rules. Alwar Rickshaw Mazdur Union's office is on Aerodrome Road. This union is primarily that of owners comprising 45 members. Currently, both these unions are involved in getting I-cards made for the drivers. They also help drivers when the need arises and apprise the authorities of their problems now and then. The rickshaw stand at the Alwar bus terminal displays a board saying—Alwar Zila Rickshaw Chalak Mazdur Union, Alwar (Rajasthan) (CITU-Lal Jhanda affiliated). According to this board, the president of this union is Sampat Ram Suraiya and its secretary is Somnath. We do not have any other information about this union. Between 1988 to 1991, the Hind Mazdur Kisan Panchayat associated Alwar Zila Rickshaw Chalak Sangh was very active here. At that time there was a license system for rickshaws in the city. This association helped 125 drivers to get bank-loans for buying rickshaws.

According to Omprakash Kochchar, 'In 1986 our Alwar rickshaw Mazdur union created a stir against the rampant corruption in the license process. Although the license fee was Rs. 23, around Rs. 200 were spent in getting the rickshaw passed. Our organisation became inactive once the system was abolished.' No matter how active the unions might have been in the past, their activities are negligible in Alwar nowadays.

It is clear from the survey of rickshaw unions in NCR that all the people associated with the rickshaw business are not alike. The concerns of owners, drivers, mechanics, passengers and producers are all different. In many ways these people complement one another yet there is a clash of interests. There is no support from the government and the rickshaw business has been declared illegal. Due to this situation, the presence of several rickshaw-owners in certain areas becomes illegal too. On paper only a physically challenged person or a widow is allowed to owb five rickshaws yet in practice this is also untrue. It is dangerous to personally own rickshaws. Concerned officials find many loopholes and discourage personal ownership by filing cases against owners thus making it difficult to believe in the motto '*Rickshaw chalak apne rickshe ka malik ho*' (Let the rickshaw-driver be the owner of his vehicle).

On the other hand, if their pockets have been sufficiently warmed then these officials encourage owners to keep the maximum number of rickshaws. However, they try to maintain control over the owners through the instrument of law. One has heard that in the capital city district, owners possess thousands of rickshaws and wish that they had legal sanction to run their business. Therefore, owners form unions to fight red-tapism. Since they have been declared illegal, they carry on their struggle in the name of drivers' union or employees' union. But at places where the owners are aware of their rights, their unions

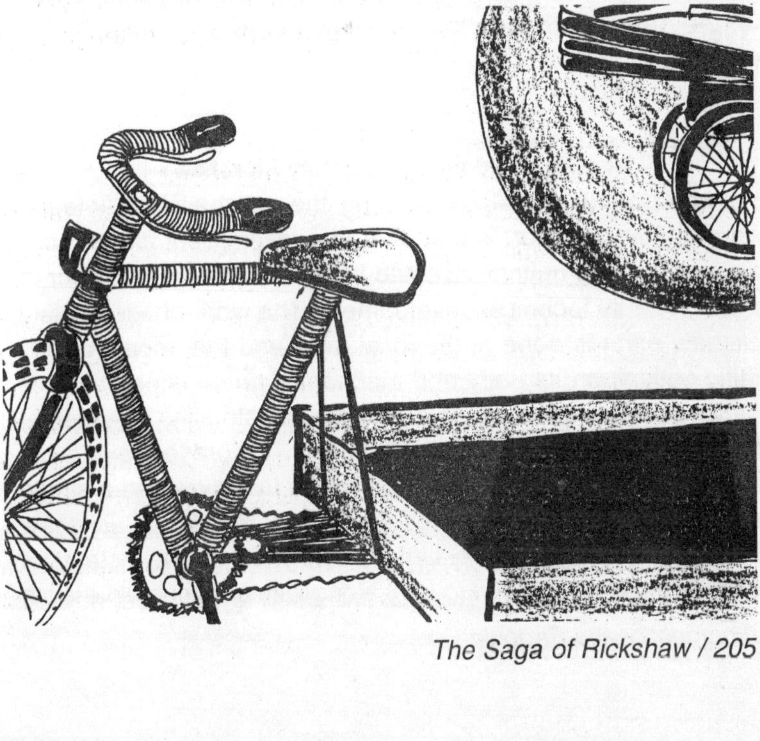

do exist and the Meerut Rickshaw Swami Sangathan is an apt example in this case.

In this entire district, unions have not developed in all the cities. In some cities where unions exist they are that of the owners or drivers but not of mechanics and passengers. Therefore there is no platform for the latter groups where they can voice their concerns.

As the number of people associated with the rickshaw business is insufficient to influence the vote bank in electoral alliances, these people are insignificant for political parties. It is a different matter that due to personal contacts, at times, owners manage to convince leaders to speak about their issues. But these ministers often forget what they say in the meetings and life goes on as usual. It is only due to the contemporary debate on environment that discussions on cycles and rickshaws in India have become common. People related to the rickshaw business agree that if they remain united then they will be able to put across their problems to the government more convincingly. The media and private organisations can play a vital role in sensitising the public about their plight. It is only in this way that the groups linked to the rickshaw will ever manage to get their rights.

II

Who will Build the 21st Century Rickshaw?

The worst result of not considering the rickshaws an integral part of public transport is that both the government and the private sector have neither invested in rickshaw production nor in research for its technical development. The work of assembling rickshaw parts is done at the local level and the impact of scientific outlook on its body and mechanics remains partial. This has an adverse effect on its durability and stability. The weight of a cycle-rickshaw is around 80–90 kg. The presence of a big frame, a loose seat, a single break in the front tyre and a single gear in the rear tyres makes the job of pulling a rickshaw extremely tiring and unsafe. Unfortunately, the informal status of being illegal and opaque industry along with administrative sloth have been instrumental in discouraging improvements in the structure of a cycle-rickshaw. If our government officials and planners accept that the rickshaw is a pollution-free, cheap and efficient mode of public transport that can provide employment to several lakh people then it is possible that the present condition of rickshaw-drivers will improve.

Even the assistant commissioner of police in Delhi, Sanjay Beniwal agrees that the traditional design of the rickshaw should be altered. It should be more stable and work-efficient. A driver must always remember that a rickshaw is one of the most unsafe modes of transport - for him as well as for the passenger sitting behind him. Thus, he should strictly follow traffic rules and always keep to his left. The tyre guard must have a blinker, dianuma reflector and a bell. The brakes should be in good condition and if possible in a shimmering cover at night so that the rickshaw is visible from a distance.

Rickshaws ply in most of the areas of NCR. The ratio of their number may be more or less when compared to population figures but there are very few area which produce rickshaws. Till now rickshaws were produced in these places in the traditional manner using the wooden body. But recently some new kind of rickshaws can be spotted having a metal-pipe body and these have recently been launched by some town although Meerut is the first city that started producing the traditional rickshaw body. The emergence of other areas as producers of new types of rickshaws has caused a setback to the Meerut rickshaw-producing industry. The number of traditional rickshaw producers has also increased challenging the veterans in this field to hold their ground. For several years, the producers have been making rickshaws according to an existing model and have not ventured into its technical research. The main reason behind this is lack of investment and even the government does not encourage them in this project. Some producers did develop new models of rickshaws for foreign buyers but they did not attempt anything for the Indian market. They believe that the drivers and owners of our country desire cheap rickshaws. Research work involves a lot of money and if it is carried out then ultimately the load will fall on the buyers who themselves will be incapable of bearing it. Thus different models of rickshaws have not been developed to date.

The rickshaw producing industry is a part of small-scale industries. In each unit only 5–10 people work and in some units all the workers are members of the same family. The introduction of offset printing machines has thrown the painters out of job in the rickshaw business. Producers buy all the things needed for manufacturing rickshaws cheap from the market and prepare rickshaws only on order. They do not make a single vehicle without demand. Therefore rickshaw production is not done through the same market mechanism under which other consumer products are manufactured. Rickshaw production is related to the customer in a more visible manner and the role of middlemen here is almost negligible.

Some financiers are buying rickshaws from producers and delivering them to owners or drivers. Similarly, some owners too are buying rickshaws on instalments and selling them to drivers on the same basis. Despite all this, rickshaw production is still not being controlled by the invisible powers of the market. Transport polices have a far-reaching influence on it. If the rickshaw manages to get government support and encouragement then there are fair chances that this industry will show some development.

A New Rickshaw Despite Consumerism

Those studying the technological development of the rickshaw believe that the growth of consumerism in the 1980s and the 1990s is under serious scrutiny now because this process has raised pertinent questions regarding the survival of life on the planet. Consumerism, over-consumption, unlimited refuse production and pollution are some of the consequences of our dependence on oil resources which may not prove long-lasting sources of energy. These fuels have generated excessive pollution which is extremely harmful to all forms of life. Therefore, at the beginning of a new millenium, the western world is turning towards the developing nations to keep environmental perspectives in mind and suggest reliable and durable alternatives. Cycle-rickshaw is one such alternative. It is a popular mode of transport in the entire Asia region especially in the Indian subcontinent.

It is surprising that while the west is looking for such sustainable options, Asian governments are ignoring them. What is even more saddening is that they are determined to get rid of these alternatives. It is indeed a critical situation where instead of making the cycle-rickshaw a more comfortable and user-friendly vehicle, we (chasing false notions of a modernised lifestyle) are bent on destroying it.

According to historical evidence, the cycle rickshaw was used for the first time in India in the 5th decade of the last century. This rickshaw was seen as a major development when compared to the rickshaws with wooden tyres or the hand-pulled rickshaws that existed at that time (in fact, the latter can still be easily seen in Kolkata.) The change in rickshaws brought about a new dignity to the profession because in the altered circumstances, a rickshaw-wallah was referred to as a driver and

not a puller. The phrase rickshaw-puller is still used but only in the context of rickshaws literally pulled by hand. Traditional cycle rickshaws can be seen in all parts of India and if observed closely, they display a lot of dissimilarities. Some have less width while others have more, some rickshaws have a top while others are roofless. Moreover, the way these rickshaws are decorated varies from place to place. But despite these differences these is a commonality of design that binds them together. Most of the rickshaws are uncomfortable and unsafe. Yet they are being widely used and in many small towns and villages, they seem to be the only mode of transport.

Three Parts of Rickshaw:
Three Segments of its Production

The structure of an ordinary cycle rickshaw can be broadly defined by describing its three parts—the cycle frame in the front, lower angle iron chassis and the wooden passenger seat. This basic structure is generally assembled with the help of nut and bolts. Then other parts like the tyre and the handle are screwed into this structure.

Similarly, the production of a rickshaw is also divided in three groups. The 1st group comprises industries that produce those complex parts on a large scale in which special attention needs to be given to measurements. For instance, handle, chair pulley and the cycle frame in the front—although these machine parts are used in cycles too yet their width is increased when they are prepared for rickshaws. The deciding factor in the sale of these parts is their weight. The more the weight of a part, the better it is considered. When the basic structure is joint with nut-bolts, it is not only loose but is also unable to hold the parts in their proper places. This makes the rickshaw unstable and the rickshaw-driver has to over-exert while pedaling. The black roadster cycle frame in the front is also big when compared to an average Indian's built. This frame is being used since the time of the Britishers and no attempt has ever been made to alter it to suit the Indian physique.

The following are the problems faced by rickshaw passengers: The passenger seat is made of thick wooden boards that are joined together with nails. Despite being heavy, this structure is weak and does not last long. The small passenger seat filled with spring, jute or coil is slightly tilted towards the front and is extremely uncomfortable on which the poor passenger has to sit in an awkward posture. Since in the entire vehicle there is no suspension system, it is enough to cause a bad backache. Moreover, it is highly unsafe for the passenger to sit in this position. The seat is removable and in case of a big jerk it can simply throw the passenger on the ground which can result in serious injury. The distance of the passenger seat from the ground is around 1 metre and the footrest is at around half a metre which makes it difficult for a passenger (especially for old people and women) to climb it.

Weak and Inferior Production

The rickshaw seat needs repair every few months and the entire structure does not last for more than 2–3 years. Because of poor construction, the vehicle no longer remains easy to handle and becomes less efficient too. The fact that there is only one gear in the rickshaw means that the rickshaw-driver has to put in more energy while driving it. Compared to the weight of an average cycle, the weight of a traditional rickshaw is much more (around 80 kg). Therefore it appears absurd that the same gear ratio should be kept for both a cycle and a rickshaw. In the absence of a multi-gear system, the rickshaw-driver himself serves as the gear box in trying to manage the rickshaw according to the changes in the condition of the road. This obviously tires him and has an adverse effect on his health.

Though it was a welcome change to have the cycle rickshaw in place of the hand-rickshaw, it is disheartening to see the traditional rickshaw in the same condition that it used to be in several years back. It isn't that efforts have not been made in this direction but attempts that have been made are very few. Trapped in various reports and files, these endeavours have never been converted into ground realities. The designers of ICRIP (Cycle-Rickshaw Improvement Project) in India attempted a completely new project in this field which started with their concern over the ill-effects that air pollution was having on the Taj Mahal in Agra. This work was initiated by the New York based ITDP (Institute for Trasport and Development Policy) in co-operation with some Indian organisations and it was funded by USAID (US Agency for International Development) along with other agencies. The focal point of the plan was to construct a modern cycle-rickshaw that would not only control the growing menace of pollution but also lay foundations for further development of the traditional rickshaw. In the present scenario this conventional rickshaw is basically in danger due to the inefficiency of its structure.

New Design

After three years of research and experimentation, the design team finally developed a modern cycle rickshaw. They claim it is a 21st century product in the truest sense. They also emphasize that the entire design process included the opinions of people associated with rickshaws (like rickshaw-drivers, passengers, producers and mechanics) and wasn't confined to the four walls of the research centre. Even people from the tourism industry were consulted. The result of this research can be used everywhere now.

According to the design team, the new rickshaw is safe for both rickshaw-drivers and passengers and in this manner it is indeed a revolutionary change. Through an integrated tubular (hollow) frame the weight has been brought down by 30 per cent (the weight of the new rickshaw is 55 kg.) and the multi-gear facility has made driving the rickshaw a convenient thing. The structural specifications of the tubular frame are also good. While driving the new rickshaw, a rickshaw-driver will have to exert less and will be able to cover more distance in less time. The gravitational centre has been lowered by one-third and this has made the rickshaw more stable. Independent studies done on rickshaw-drivers using modern rickshaws (there are about 300 of them) reveal that the time for which these vehicles can be driven has gone up by one-third. This has also led to an average increase in the rickshaw-drivers income by 60 per cent. Another reason for the growth in income could be the comfortable seats which are tied on top of the tubular frame by nylon strips. Thus it is safer and easier to sit in a rickshaw which also has a good suspension now due to which jerks can be avoided. A lower foot-rest, a place to keep things and a roof to protect the passenger from sunlight and rain are some other advantages because of which the passenger readily pays more money. Some of the factors that were kept in mind while developing the design of the rickshaw were labour, road security, maintenance and longevity. An important part of this plan has been the role played by the business sector and perhaps due to it the project has been so successful. While developing the design, attention was paid not only to the nature of the rickshaw industry but also to how well the design will fit into the present system. In the modern rickshaw most of the parts of the traditional rickshaw industry have been retained. Parts like the tyre and the handle are still being made by the old industry. The only new aspect is frame production. The production of a separate cycle frame would become redundant. The work of rickshaw assembly is still with the old workers-mechanics who also act as sellers and

financers. In the new integrated frame, various parts can be fitted better and this has reduced the complexity of the structure. A major change has come in the industries that earlier produced angle iron chassis, other metal parts and wooden frames. Now they will have to make integrated frames.

As the design team highlights, the main idea behind the entire enterprise was not to make a technically superior and complex rickshaw which would be out of reach for most of the people. Instead the emphasis was to develop an easy and efficient cycle rickshaw using the appropriate technique. Since the rickshaw industry will remain a part of small-scale industries, it will provide many jobs. ICRIP wishes to popularise this rickshaw not only in places where it was already in use but also in areas where rickshaws have never been driven. This complete change in the rickshaw and its beautification is in keeping with the fast changing scenario of today.

May be after these developments the rickshaw will no longer be considered an inferior and unsafe vehicle that offend the human dignity. It will be in accordance with the environment and will be more profitable for rickshaw-wallahs and passengers alike. Increased income will also raise the living standard of the rickshaw-driver—something he has always dreamt of. Moreover, these rickshaws will also bring about a change in the attitude of those who scorned at the sight of a rickshaw since now it is safe, comfortable as well as more attractive. Considering the present-day unsatisfactory public transport system, rickshaws provide a cheap and convenient transport facility. As it is one of the main modes of transport in small towns and villages, rickshaws are bound to remain on the stage for times to come.

The survey conducted by the Jan Parivahan Panchayat on rickshaw technology has revealed that in the entire Delhi district, improvements are desired in the traditional rickshaw for the benefit of rickshaw-drivers and passengers. However, among rickshaw-mechanics only 13.8 per cent are in favour of technical changes in the vehicle and 86.2 per cent believe that no improvements are needed. Out of all the people in support of changes, 46.2 per cent mechanics talk about alterations in the tup, the mudguard and the roof of the rickshaw, 7.7 per cent emphasize improvements in the bell, 34.6 per cent mechanics talk of comfortable seats and 11.5 per cent recommend some other kind of technical change.

All the mechanics are not aware of the fact that the new rickshaw has reached to the NCR: 10.6 per cent have not heard about it while 42.3 per cent have seen it, 1.1 per cent of mechanics have used it and 46 per cent have no knowledge about it. In order to execute a repair work, proper training is required. Thus, 79.9 per cent mechanics of the district desire professional training but 20.1 per cent do not since they think whatever they know is enough for them.

Jan Parivahan Panchayat asked some questions from rickshaw-owners in the area regarding the wooden body. One of the questions was—do you think there is any need for improvement in the present rickshaw? 93.8 per cent owners answered in the negative. Only 6.2 per cent said yes. When we asked for suggestions, various owners advocated changes in different parts: 21 per cent emphasised on good quality parts, 52.6 per cent suggested putting tup, mudguard and roof and 21 per cent voted in favour of comfortable seats 5.3 per cent owners suggested other improvements.

We also asked the owners of the capital city about the new model of the rickshaw: 48.7 per cent of them said that they had seen it but 34.4 per cent said they had us idea about it. Only 16.2 per cent owners had heard about the new model. In the Haryana district, 1.5 per cent owners said they had driven this rickshaw themselves, 98.4 per cent of them told us that they had got no benefits from the government while 2.3 per cent accept availing the bank-loan facility.

Should the rickshaw business be given the status of small industry? The owners are divided into 3 sections on this question. 6.05 per cent say that it should not be included in small industries, 87.3 per cent advocate the inclusion of rickshaw business in small-scale industries and 6.2 per cent are unsure of their viewpoint. When asked whether they were willing to give a guarantee or residential proof certificate to get a license made for their rickshaw-drivers, 38.6 per cent said no and 61.4 per cent answered in the affirmative.

Rickshaw Technology and Its Journey

Newspapers of October 1999 and July 2000 screamed that the new rickshaw technology had come to India and soon the new rickshaws would begin plying on the roads of Agra and Delhi. In the 28 October 1999 issue of 'Amar Ujala' Hindi newspaper, the photograph of the new rickshaw was published along with the caption—just wait for another day. Tomorrow (that is on 29 October) the rickshaws produced with the new technology will begin being driven in front of the Taj Mahal. Both environment and the passenger will be safe now.

Indeed on the designated day, four dozen rickshaws appeared in front of the Taj Mahal. They were different from the traditional rickshaws in many ways. Their weight was less than that of the traditional rickshaws by 25 kg. And wood or solid metal was used nowhere in them. One look at these rickshaws makes it clear why it is special—the passenger seat and the backrest is woven with cotton tape making it comfortable and leaving more scope for the air to pass. The umbrella on top of the seat provides shelter from sunlight and rain. There is space under the seat to keep things. The seat is wider and the foot-rest is lower enabling the passenger to climb the rickshaw comfortably. The chassis of this rickshaw has a lower centre of gravity so that the possibility of the vehicle turning upside down is ruled out. The multigear facility enables the rickshaw-driver to take the rickshaw uphill without exerting himself. Compared to the traditional rickshaw, this rickshaw is costlier by a few hundred rupees.

These rickshaws were inaugurated in a function held on 10 July, 2000 by Delhi's Chief Minister, Sheila Dikshit, 20 new rickshaws were launched that day and 200 more were promised to hit the roads soon. In her address, the chief minister said—'Rickshaw suits the environment since it does not use fuel and is pollution-free. Apart from saving fuel, the rickshaw enables us

to save foreign investment. Since 75 per cent of pollution is spread by motorized vehicles in the city, our government is in favour of encouraging the rickshaws. The drivers of modern rickshaw will not face any difficulty in getting the license. *(Jansatta, Delhi, 11 July 2000).*

The modern rickshaw was prepared by two non-government organisations, Institute for Transportation and Development Policy, New York and Asian Institute for Transport Development, New Delhi along with the support of Indian Institute of Technology, Delhi. But this research for a new technology is not the only one of this kind. Earlier, Delhi engineer C. P. Bhatnagar had produced a new model of rickshaw by the name of Iko Tryke. This rickshaw had seating space for three adults and had all the special features present in the modern rickshaw. It has a small chain which made it easier to drive. The presence of rubber pieces in the vehicle helped it to sustain jerks. It has brakes in the front as well as at the back. Since the rear tyres are that of a moped, the rickshaw is capable of lifting heavy luggage. Thirty-five Iko Tryke rickshaws are ready to ply on Delhi roads and are waiting to get the license from the Delhi Municipal Corporation. The responsibility for these rickshaws has been taken up by Nirman Mazdur Panchayat Sangam. It is difficult to predict the fate of these rickshaws. Referring to them, '*Sandhay Times*', New Delhi had given them this title in its 7 August 1997 issue—'Conforming to the necessity of time and our country, here comes a new rickshaw. Voicing the opinion of Centre for Technology and Development's C. P. Bhatnagar, the newspaper had written—'Today's unsafe and polluted environment poses a great threat to human life and nature. It is strange that in order to stop this phenomenon, the government is showing no interest. It has made the production of cars (motorised vehicles) license-free but in the case of rickshaws (pollution-free vehicles), restrictions regarding license and limited number are being put. Had these rickshaws got licenses earlier, they would have been plying on the roads by now.'

No one can understand the hardships of a rickshaw-driver better than the driver himself. Sheikh Jabbar of Nagpur became a rickshaw-mechanic after working as a rickshaw-driver. In order to make the job of pulling a rickshaw less stressful, he invented the rickshaw with two gears. By placing the brakes in the rear tyres, he also made the rickshaw more safe. Sheikh Jabbar produced the two-gear rickshaw in 1988, a three-gear rickshaw in 1991 and a four-gear vehicle in 1995. In the 20 July, 2000 issue of '*Jansatta*', New Delhi, Anil Pandey wrote—'Around five years back, the reputed technician and Gandhian, Binu Kaley took government help and got 24 two-gear rickshaws made from Jabbar and distributed them amongst people. This work could not be carried forth due to lack of money. Since Jabbar did not have an engineering degree, the government and other organisations did not give him any preference.'

Whatever significant inventions have taken place till date have some inventor's name attached to them. But unfortunately, Sheikh Jabbar who conceptualised the rickshaw with gears in India is known to no one. Jabbar belongs to a traditional weaver family. Initially Jabbar worked as a weaver but when the age of mechanisation threatened their profession, he was forced to hunt for an alternative means of livelihood. In order to provide two meals for his family, Jabbar bought an old cycle-rickshaw and began driving it.

But his already frail body could not go on for long and he fell ill. It was only during his illness that Jabbar realised that although a lot of energy is spent in driving a rickshaw, there is hardly any money earned. Thus, he started thinking in terms of how this process could be made simpler. Jabbar involved himself in producing a new kind of rickshaw but he had no resources. He collected things from junk-dealers and started experimenting.

Jabbar opened a rickshaw repairing shop through which he not only earned some money but also found time to research. He spent the next 15 years experimenting with his limited resources. Despite initial failures, he carried on. His relatives started taunting him but he remained undeterred. Finally in 1989, Jabbar succeeded and made his invention public. Now Jabbar bhai has put four gears in his rickshaw and brakes in the rear tyres making it faster and safer. This has built his self-confidence and made him more ambitious. In 1992, Professor Yashpal had shown Jabbar Bhai's invention on Doordarshan's national programme 'Turning Point'. But despite these efforts, Jabbar Bhai is still in search for true recognition. To gather public support he has travelled the 200 km. stretch from Nagpur to Vardha several times. He has also travelled to Delhi on his rickshaw in connection with his experiment.

Various attempts have been made in our country and abroad for the development of a new technology for a rickshaw. Several research works have been conducted in the IITs of Mumbai, Kanpur and Chennai as well as in district and state level engineering colleges, universities, research centres and non-government organisations. But these research projects have not benefited people from the rickshaw business. Instead they have been reduced to mere academic exercises that have remained inside the boundaries of research labs. Their use has not gone beyond getting degrees and scholarships for the concerned researchers. People who have made an attempt to let public benefit from these experiments have got no financial or legal help from the government. The result was that the rickshaw industry kept moving at its own pace. If the government emphasises on new technology and provides financial and legal security to rickshaw-drivers, owners and researchers, there is no doubt that better models of rickshaws will be produced. This will not only solve the problem of pollution but also encourage self-employment.

Two years after the inauguration of the new rickshaws in Delhi, another rickshaw with a new design has become popular and can be seen mainly in the Karol Bagh and Mayur Vihar regions of the city though one or two of them may be found in other areas too. These rickshaws are not modern rickshaws. They are different from traditional rickshaws only in the sense of being more fancy. Thus, the nouveau-riche do not hesitate to sit in them. By putting a little more money in these rickshaws, the owners can charge more rent from the rickshaw-drivers. This new vehicle is actually the traditional rickshaw with a metal-pipe body. It has no advantage for the rickshaw-driver either financially or physically. However, producers of wooden bodies are in great danger. But this was bound to happen once the new technology was given a green signal. Why is there so much reluctance in accepting it? The reason is government policies and a lack of co-ordination between the material condition of new research work and the rickshaw industry. The result is that the owner invests only that much of money which keeps the rickshaw in a working condition. After all, there is a danger of the rickshaw being confiscated and broken. Why should he waste his money? The rickshaw-driver has no place in this business. He usually drives a rented rickshaw. If he were to ask for a modern rickshaw, he would find himself jobless. People who develop the rickshaws do not maintain a living relationship with the people of this business. They are not concerned about how people will tackle problems that might arise in future in the rickshaws that they develop. They do not show the determination to be involved in their research work for long. Therefore any new technique is also sacrificed in favour of the traditional structure. All is left in the hands of God.

One can conclude by saying that the research conducted for the technological improvement of rickshaws has not come to the fore as a ground reality. Therefore, the technology of modern rickshaws has not become a successful alternative to the traditional rickshaw. A new model has been developed by mixing the techniques. This new rickshaw has been made by placing a metallic body on the Y-chassis of the traditional rickshaw. In fact, for the rickshaw-driver this version is even heavier than the traditional rickshaw. There is no special work for mechanics in this rickshaw. Of course, the owners have got a reason to demand more rent from rickshaw-drivers as they have put in more money in these vehicles. New technology for rickshaws can definitely be developed if Indian brains are encouraged. But Sheikh Jabbar's case proves how talent in dying in the country. The government should extend financial help to producers and mechanics so that they feel inspired to work on technological advances of the rickshaws. Moreover, favourable policies must be framed and competition should be encouraged. Technological improvements can only become a practical reality when the government gives legal sanction to the rickshaw business and makes relevant changes in policies so that rickshaw-owners and rickshaw-drivers are pressurised into accepting the new technology. The government should also welcome every new model of the rickshaw so that there is a healthy competition between producers and they feel motivated to introduce technological changes. Maybe some of these models will be used by people as personal pollution-free vehicles. Everyone will benefit from the technological development of rickshaws. Rickshaw-drivers will find it easy to drive these rickshaws and passengers will find it comfortable to sit in. Producers will find work and owners will get more money. Colourful rickshaws will adorn the roads and will provide aesthetic pleasure to lovers of beauty.

THREE

Rikshaw and its Claims

Suggestions and Recommendations

Compared to other Indian cities, Delhi has the maximum number of motor vehicles. Along with this, the number of cycle rickshaws and other non-motorised vehicles in the city is also on the rise. Though there is a growth in income standards and the number of cars and scooters has also shot up, it is hard to deny that there is an equal demand for cycles, rickshaws and carts too. The rise in non-motorised vehicles is taking place in a scenario where the traffic-control policies are against them and the roads are being constructed keeping the convenience of cars in mind. Given the socio-economic structure of the population and the geographical situation of the city, there is a fair chance that the condition will remain the same in the future as well. Therefore it becomes necessary to demand that such policies and basic structures be developed that enable a smooth movement of cycle rickshaws. It needs no mention that amidst the heavy pollution traffic of Delhi, the cycle rickshaw is a pollution free vehicle and a convenient mode of transport for short distances.

In the entire NCR, rickshaw-drivers do not have any facility at the government level. Almost all these rickshaw-drivers (97 per cent) agree that there should be a separate lane on the road for vehicles like rickshaws. Barring 2–3 per cent rickshaw-drivers, the rest emphasize that there should be separate stands and parking areas for them. The present day policies are a hindrance for rickshaws and other non-motorised vehicles since they are based on the wrong belief that an efficient transport system has no place for such vehicles. Therefore in Delhi, traffic control experts and traffic police have put all kinds of restrictions on rickshaws with respect to time and place.

In order to control the number of rickshaws in the city, the government has fixed the upper limit of registered rickshaws at 99,000. A person needs a valid ration card to avail the license which is not made throughout the year but only during certain months. But such obstructive policies ought to be viewed in the context of the current globalised economy. Every other day where the highest policy-makers reiterate that for the economy to effectively function, less government controls need to be exercised, shouldn't the same yard-stick be applicable to cycle rickshaws and other vehicles in this category? It is often expected of a good road network to cater well to the need of all kinds of road-users but in a mixed traffic situation, pedestrians and cycle and rickshaw-drivers need most attention.

Until and unless attention is paid to the needs of this class, the rest of the modes of transport will also remain less efficient. In formulating a safe and sustainable model of traffic system, two things must be kept in mind: On roads with more than 30 metre ROW, there should be a separate lane for cycles, rickshaws etc. where motorised vehicles especially two-wheelers should be prohibited from entering. On roads with ROW less than 30 m, traffic control rules should be taken help of and average speed should be kept below 20-30 kms. per hour.

Roads in Delhi have not been systematically utilised. Zebra

crossings, pedestrian crossings and over-bridges that have been constructed for the benefit of pedestrians have not been located at appropriate places. The net result is that people do not use them at all. These facilities must be provided near bus stops. Moreover, there should also be a provision for cycle and rickshaw repair-work and parking. At a time when fast-moving traffic and a clean environment has become everyone's concern, it is not possible to ignore the importance of the rickshaw and other non-motorised vehicles in the modern transport system. And when their basic needs and structural concerns are ignored, they unintentionally create chaos and disorder

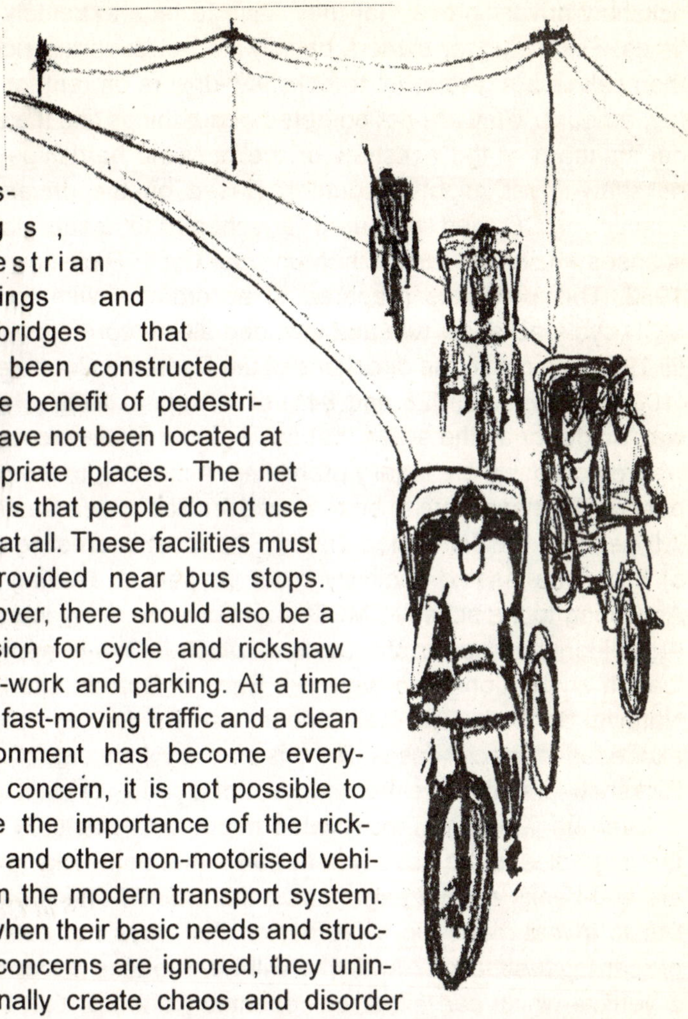

for the rest of the vehicles. The government generally encourages policies that hinder and obstruct these slow-moving vehicles. It is quite feasible to have adequate facilities for cycles and rickshaws etc. on roads and parking lots. This step will also facilitate a smooth functioning of other vehicles.

Another factor that goes in favour of cycle rickshaws is employment enrichment. Rickshaws provide jobs to several displaced workers. Many studies that have been conducted on rickshaw-drivers prove that they have to face extremely trying times. For instance, owners usually do not drive the rickshaw themselves but give them to rickshaw-drivers on rent for a certain amount. They are not bothered about things like the technical standard of the rickshaw or the possible hardships that a rickshaw-driver might encounter. Based on the driver-owner concept, MCD had prepared a scheme to issue rickshaw licenses known as the Delhi Municipal Cycle Rickshaw Policy 1982. This plan was prepared in accordance with the 1960 MCD cycle rickshaw rule and included all the corrections made till 1976 along with the directions of the Supreme Court decision (1989's CWP-no's. 728 and 841) of 5 August, 1980. This plan was made for all the areas that come under MCD except those where rickshaws are legally prohibited. According to the plan 15 per cent licenses were to be reserved for Scheduled Castes and 7.5 per cent for Scheduled Tribes. The most interesting aspect of this was issuing eligibility-proof for people desiring loans. According to the scheme, MCD would provide every loan-seeker an identity proof on the basis of which he could apply for a loan in any nationalised bank like Bank of Baroda and Punjab National Bank etc. The loan amount was Rs. 900 and could be exceeded in special cases. But this plan is visible only on paper. Rickshaw-drivers are either unaware of it or do not want to avail it. Even banks are not too excited about it. It is actually due to the loopholes in the government policy that both rickshaw-drivers and banks are not eager about the project. Which bank will like to invest money in a profession that does not even have proper legal sanction? And who will want to take a loan to buy a vehicle which can either be repeatedly fined or can be broken/destroyed any day.

The rickshaw is the most convenient and cheap vehicle of public transport that drops the passenger at his doorstep. It does not need petrol, it causes no pollution and it does not require much space. Like DTC and taxi drivers, rickshaw-drivers too should be considered transport employees in the category of non-motorised vehicles. The government has declared that along with the help of the planning commission, an inte-

grated transport policy will be prepared. A lot of effort has been made to draw the attention of the government towards the fact that if rickshaws are not included in this plan, then instead of being an integrated scheme it will merely be an automobile policy. Due to the obstructions created for non-motorized vehicles and the prohibitions levelled on them, the element of self-sufficiency in our transport process is fast disappearing and we are becoming slaves of vehicles run on fuel. By creating a new department of non-motorised vehicles cycles, rickshaws, carts and pedestrians etc. can be included in it. For the poor rickshaw-wallah, there is still no respite from the license system therefore it is pertinent that license laws be altered in his favour. On the other hand, traffic police ought to pay special attention to the convenience of cycle, rickshaw-drivers and pedestrians. The most significant point is that in the entire Delhi district, not just the number of rickshaws but the number of all vehicles ought to be fixed. The transport policy must ensure that non-motorised vehicles will get their proper share on the road. The entire category should be treated as a non-polluting industry and should be encouraged by being provided subsidies. People using rickshaws should also get an allowance. It is a contradiction that on the one hand, our planners talk of controlling pollution and on the other hand, they make no noticeable effort to unite or strengthen the vehicles in the pollution-free category. There is no doubt that the rickshaw can play a very important role in the transport system of the city.

In today's changed circumstances, the significance of rickshaws is growing day by day. Its relevance in Indian society's economic and social background is undeniable. Based on an analysis of the facts discovered during the detailed study on rickshaws conducted by Jan Parivahan Panchayat, the following recommendations can be made:

(1) Rickshaws should be considered an integral part of the public transport system. Thus, new provisions need to be made for the development of the rickshaw and other non-motorised vehicles. Rickshaws ought to be encouraged in order to control pollution in the city and hence, relevant changes in rules and regulations must be brought about. There should be facilities provided to rickshaw-wallahs at hospitals and health centres. An important point in the policies formulated in future has to be the eradication of a rickshaw-driver's poverty. Democratic control should be exercised only when all the vehicles plying in an area are viewed within the framework of a integerated transport system. It will be harmful to be biased in favour of a particular vehicle. All the rickshaw related laws should be analysed afresh and altered whereever necessary. Prohibitions on plying rickshaws on Delhi roads should be removed. Being helpful to the weaker sections of society as well as being environment-friendly, rickshaws should be supported in every way. There must be a separate lane on wide roads for non-motorised vehicles. Narrow roads and public places should be reserved exclusively for entry of rickshaws. License system for rickshaws should be abolished and a registration method (like in the case of motorised vehicles) should be introduced. The process of confiscating and breaking rickshaws should be stopped. Rickshaw-drivers must be informed about traffic rules time and again and proper training must be imparted to them. In accordance with the popula-

tion of the city, a friendly rickshaw network plan should be formulated.

(2) All the people associated with the rickshaw business must be provided bank-loans and insurance facilities. A rickshaw co-operative society ought to be formed for temporary drivers and basic necessities like shelter, toilets and bathrooms should be arranged for them. Placing rickshaw business in the category of small-scale industries, required help should be given to the owners and producers. Rickshaw stands should be constructed near bus-stands and parking areas. Considering rickshaw as a pollution-free public vehicle, all kinds of tax rebates should be offered to its users.

(3) A government policy must be formulated on the technological development of a rickshaw and budgetary provisions must be made at all levels. In programmes related to technological development, importance must be given to the role played by rickshaw producers, mechanics, research institutes and non-government organisations. Rickshaw-mechanics should be given suitable places to carry on their repair work and owners too should be provided with appropriate locations for their garages. They can be asked to pay a tax or a fixed amount of money for this favour. Training ought to be given to rickshaw-mechanics too. Rickshaw-drivers and mechanics should be saved from police atrocities and harassment from bad elements of society.

(4) In order to popularise the rickshaw, a social-level propaganda programme must be carried out and related programmes should be held. To make those people connected with the rickshaw business more conscious and aware seminars, exhibitions, fairs and demonstrations should be organised at the local and district levels. Last but not the least, night schools should be opened to make rickshaw-drivers literate.

References and Bibliography

Books and Reports

1. *Cycle Rickshaw in National Capital Region: Data Book*, Jan Parivahan Panchayat, Lokayan, 13-Alipur Road, Delhi-54.
2. *Rashtriya Rajdhani Parikshetra ka Cycle Rickshaw* and *Rickshaw Pullers 2000–2002*, Jan Parivahan Panchayat, Lokayan Publication, 13-Alipur Road, Delhi.
3. Articles related to Rickshaw-wallahs published in Madhu Kishwar's *Manushi*: See *Manushi,* Vol. 125, 126, 134 and 135.
4. Rajendra Ravi's article : '*Cycle Rickshaw Par Punarvichar*', August, 2001.
5. Book published by Jan Parivahan Panchayat: *Pradhan mantri ka khat / kitna naya: kitna udar (Delhi mein Cycle Rickshaw Vaikalpik Niti Ka Praroop)*.
6. Tony Wheeler and Richard Aianson, *Chasing Rickshaws*, Lonely Planet Publications, Australia, 1998.
7. N. Vittal, 'A vision for new India', A presentation at the Bharat Vikas Parishad, Chennai on 24 October, 2001.
8. Suresh Pandit, *Alwar: Kal, Aaj aur Ka*l, Alwar Vichar Manch, Alwar.
9. *Chavni Adhiniyam, 1924*, Niyantrak, Bharat Sarkar, Civil Lines, Delhi-54.
10. Khushwant Singh, *Delhi*, Kitab Ghar, New Delhi.
11. Maheshwar Dayal, *Delhi Jo Ek Shahar Hai*, Hindi Academy, New Delhi.
12. Kannan Jheengan, *Dareenchon Se*, Manlik Sahitya Prakashan, Delhi-7.

13. *Delhi Nagar Nigam Adhiniyam, 1957*, Niyantrak, Bharat Sarkar, Civil Lines, Delhi-54.
14. *Nagrik Margdarshika: Delhi Nagar Nigam*, Town Hall, Chandni Chowk, Delhi-6.
15. *Niyam, Viniyam Tatha upvidhiyan : Nagar Palika, Bulandshahar* (Part-I), Nagar Palika, Bulandshahar.
16. Lalit Mishra 'Vatsa', *Noida Pragati (2000)*, Noida.
17. *Mela Nauchandi (1991)*, Nagar Mahapalika, Meerut.
18. Ravishankar Sharma, *Mela Nauchandi (1995)*, Nagar Nigam, Meerut.
19. Aditya Sharma (Editor), *Mela Nauchandi (1997)*, Nagar Nigam, Meerut.
20. Lao Sh, *Rickshaw-wala*, Hind Pocket Books, Delhi.
21. *Citizen's Charter and Information Booklet*, New Delhi Nagar Palika Parishad, Palika Kendra, New Delhi-1.
22. Tatsuharu Kodama, *Shin Ki Tipahiya Cycle*, Bharat Gyan-Vigyan Samiti, New Delhi-66.
23. *A Programme to Produce Films and Literature to Educate and Motivate people to follow norms and rules of the Road,* Institute for Study of Science and Social Policy, *ASB-55*, Piyush Path, Bapu Nagar, Jaipur-302004.
24. *A study on the performance of State Road Transport Undertakings—Passenger Services (1992–2000)*, Transport Research Wing, Ministry of Road Transport and Highway, February, 2001.
25. *Basic Road Statistic of India, 1996-97*, Transport Rescue Wing, Ministry of Surface Transport, Government of India, New Delhi.
26. Geoffrey Moorhouse, *Calcutta,* Penguin, New Delhi.
27. J. H. Graferd, *Carefree Cities*, International Books, Netherlands.
28. Rinki Singh, *Consumer Training Manual—4 : Road Transport and Railways*, Consumer Co-ordination Council, New Delhi.
29. Arif A. Wakif, *Co-operative Development of Transport and Communications Centre in South Asia,* Macmillan, New Delhi.

30. *Cycle Rickshaws in India (A Survey of Design and Design Factors)*, Unnayan, Calcutta.
31. *Cycling in Dutch Cities: Ten Excursions in the Netherlands*, Dutch Cyclists' Union, Uttakt.
32. Peggy Mohan, *Dealing with Traffic*, Antara Foundation, Delhi.
33. A. R. Vig, *Delhi is Dying*, Ajanta, Delhi.
34. *Delhi-Vision 2010 ; Traffic and Transport Management in Delhi*, Delhi Committee, Ph.D. Chambers of Commerce and Industry, New Delhi.
35. *Delhi Master Plan,* August 1990, Akalank Publications, Delhi.
36. *Directory on Rickshaw and Baby Taxi Painters of Bangladesh,* Alliance francais di Dhaka, Dhaka.
37. Urs Hillary, *Environmental Limits to Motorisation,* Har anand Publications, New Delhi.
38. Wolfgang Sachs, *For Love of the Automobiles,* University of California Press, Oxford, England.
39. *From Horse-drawn Omnibus to Articulated Transport,* Helsinki City Transport 1972, Published by Helsinki City Transport.
40. *Hand Rickshaws in Calcutta: Fact and Issues,* Unayan, Calcutta.
41. *Information Brochure,* New Delhi Municipal Council, New Delhi.
42. *Locating the space for Innovations in India Cycle-Rickshaw: A Review of the Efforts and the Perceptions of the Innovators, Assemblers and Pullers*, Centre for Science Technology and Environmental Policy Studies, New Delhi.
43. *Meerut Cantonment Board; Rules and Bye-laws (Framed under the Cantonment Act 1924),* Meerut Cantonment, Meerut.
44. *Motor Transport Statistics of India—1977-78,* Transport Research Wing, Ministry of Surface Transport, Government of India, New Delhi.
45. *National Capital Region Directory*, NCR Planning Board,

New Delhi.
46. *National Capital Region: Growth and Development,* NCR Planning Board, New Delhi.
47. *Neglected and Vulnerable Road User: The Pedestrian,* Institute of Road Traffic Education, New Delhi.
48. *Ninth Five-year Plan for the Transport Sector (1997–2002)*, Transport Department, Government of NCT of Delhi.
49. *Non-motorised Transport—The World Bank,* American Development Bank.
50. *Non-motorised Transport in India*, Asian Institute of Transport Development, New Delhi.
51. *Non-motorised Vehicles in 10 Asian Cities—The World Bank*, Transportation, Water and Urban Development Department, Transport Division (March, 1995).
52. V. K. Malhotra, *Patna Municipal Corporation Act, 1951*, Malhotra Brothers, Frazer Road, Patna.
53. *Pedestrian Subways*, Institute of Road Traffic Education.
54. *Rickshaw Pullers of Cuttack City : A Tentative Status Report (July 1999)*, National Institute of Applied Human Research and Development, Cuttack.
55. Jug Suraiya, *Rickshaw Ragtime*, Penguin, New Delhi.
56. Raja Bhasin, *Simla: The Summer Capital of British India,* Penguin, New Delhi.
57. *Road Accident in Delhi*, Delhi Traffic Police, Delhi.
58. M. S. Upadhyay, *Road Accidents of Delhi (1994-1998),* Deputy Commissioner of Police, Traffic, Delhi.
59. Kamal Siddiqui, Saida Roshan Quadir, Sitara Alamgir, Saidul Haq, *Social Formation in Dhaka City,* University Press Limited, Dhaka.
60. *Taking steps : A Community Action Guide to People-centred, Equitable and Sustainable Urban Transport,* The Sustran Network, Kuala Lumpur, Malaysia.
61. Jurgan Hayen-Preshan, *The Bicycle in Uganda,* Wahlterf, Germany.
62. *The Capital's Homeless*, Ashray Adhikar Abhiyan, Delhi.
63. Dominique Lapierre, *The City of Joy,* Warmer Books, New York.

64. *Delhi Municipal Corporation Act, 1957,* Akalank Publications, Delhi.
65. Ton Welman & Sons, *The Dutch Bicycle Master Plan,* Ministry of Transport Public Works and Water Management, Directorate General for Passenger Transport, The Hague.
66. Jersen Bois and Rolf Witting, *The Economic Significance of Cycling,* The Haghe.
67. Nikola Bird, *The Estate We Are In*, Indigo, London.
68. Jagdish Arora, *The Haryana Municipal Act with Rules and Bye-laws*, Singla Law Agency, Chandigarh.
69. *The Indian Railways Act, 1989,* Consumer Co-ordination Council, New Delhi.
70. *The New Delhi Municipal Council Act,* 1994, Akalank Publications, Delhi.
71. Bhagat Jeet Singh, *The Punjab Municipal Act 1911,* Chawla Publications, Chandigarh.
72. J. Chander, *The Punjab Municipal Act and Election Rules,* The Bright Law House, Delhi.
73. Catazyarna Tota, *The Role of Non-motorised Transport in Sustainable Urban Transport Systems,* Teri, New Delhi.
74. Naomi C. Casbiyan Sons, *Transportation Research Records 1294: Non-motorised Transportation, 1991,* Transportion Research Board, National Council, Washington DC, 1991.
75. *Vulnerable Road Users in Asian and Pacific Regions,* Asian Development Bank, Manila, Philippines.

Magazines and Newspapers

1. Amar Ujala (Daily), Meerut.
2. India Today (Weekly), New Delhi.
3. Jansatta (Daily), New Delhi.
4. Dainik Jaagran (Daily), New Delhi.

5. Rashtriya Sahara (Daily), New Delhi.
6. Navbharat Times (Daily), New Delhi.
7. Vinay (Alwar Issue, 1969), Rajshri College, Alwar.
8. Vir Arjun (Daily), New Delhi.
9. Sandhya Times (Daily), New Delhi.
10. Samayik Vaarta (Monthly), New Delhi.
11. Hindustan (Daily), New Delhi.
12. Asian Transport Journal, Asian Institute of Transport Development, New Delhi.
13. Down to Earth, New Delhi. (Fortnightly)
14. The Hindu (Daily), Delhi.
15. The Hindustan Times (Daily), New Delhi.
16. The Indian Express (Daily), New Delhi.
17. The Times of India (Daily), New Delhi.
18. Transport Track (July 2001), New Delhi.
19. Shramjivi, January-March 2001, New Delhi.

Photos and Illustrations

1. Photos on Pages 23, 25, 27 and 29 are from Raja Bhasin's book 'Simla: The Summer Capital of India'.

2. Photo on Page. 73 was taken by the Jan Parivahan Panchayat team.

3. Illustrations on Pages 215 and 219 are taken from the study 'Locating the space for innovations in Indian Cycle-Rickshaw: A View of the Efforts by the Perceptions of the Innovators, Assemblers and Pullers'. This study was done by the Centre for Science Technology and Environmental Policy Studies.

4. Illustration on Page. 217 is taken from a sticker published by Lokayan in 2003.

